D1737067

Authentic Tennis

BILL LEFKO
DANIEL BAIRD

ISBN: 0988364808
First edition, first printing.

Cover photo courtesy of Bianca Lazarini Forreque.

Black Mesa Publishing, LLC
Florida
Black.Mesa.Publishing@gmail.com

www.blackmesabooks.com

Authentic Tennis

CONTENTS

ACKNOWLEDGMENTS

BILL LEFKO:

There are so many knowledgeable and gifted people who have crossed my life path it would be impossible to list them all. Some will be mentioned in the introduction, but there are many more people without whom my life's purpose may not have been fulfilled. Special thanks to my wife Gayle, who has been my greatest supporter and who has been by my side through better and worse. Special thanks to my wonderful kids, Courtney and Kellie who have grown into honorable loving people. A special debt of gratitude and appreciation for my son Courtney who has taught tennis by my side for the last 14 years. Without his help, love, and support I would probably not be still on the courts. Special thanks to my dearest and closest friend Daniel Baird, whom I have worked with closely for many years to develop the Authentic philosophy, without his wisdom and his unique ability to help create a feel based book, Authentic

Tennis would probably be still just a collection of notes. Special thanks to my sister in law Oletha Meade Melland, who has helped me to create the stability that I have always longed for. Special thanks to Pam, Courtney's wife and my grand kids, Cammy and Dylan Lefko; they have been a source of constant motivation and joy in my life. Special thanks to all the tennis students who have appreciated my passion for the game, believed in my teaching approach and have supported me over the years.

DANIEL BAIRD:

A very special thanks to the love of my life Lorrie, for her unconditional love and support. Special thanks to my older brother, Sam, for looking out for my well being and introducing me to Bill and Gayle Lefko. Special thanks to my dear friend Bill Lefko who welcomed me into their home so many years ago and accepted me unconditionally, which helped me to realize that I had something valuable to offer the world. Special thanks to my good friend Clifford Burns for his creative insights into the nature of consciousness. Special thanks to my close friend Bruce Donaldson for his help and friendship over the years. Special thanks to Pat Gill for his giving spirit and his personal help in many areas of life. Special thanks to my good friend David Phillips for always lending a helping hand when I needed it. I'd like to give a special thanks to my Mom, brother Billy, sisters Theresa, and Sandra for always being there for me. Last but not least, I'd like to thank all of my students and friends who have supported me over the years through the medium of tennis.

INTRODUCTION

TENNIS IS MY CALLING—my mission from God, which has inspired the writing of this book and led to my finding of Authentic Tennis. Tennis would become my vehicle for self-discovery. I once heard a great opinion from a fellow tennis pro, "Your approach to tennis and your behavior on the tennis court is a reflection of your demeanor in life." These words stayed with me throughout my quest to find a better way and would help me understand the basic nature of the students that I would encounter.

I, Bill Lefko, started out teaching tennis traditionally using the mechanical method. My basic nature was to "know and analyze". I was in a constant search for information that would make me a better teacher and would create job stability. My perspective was that if I knew more, spent more hours on the court and gave one hundred percent all the time that stability would be the outcome. The search for stability and process would become my life struggle. I was always looking for a better way. Regardless of the information that was presented to me, it was never enough. Teaching tennis never felt easy because I was in a constant state of trying too hard. My tennis story and life experiences would be one that would move me from struggle to inspiration. Many encounters with inspirational people would mold my teaching style and life forever.

Tennis had me from the first day that I stepped onto a tennis court at age 12. I won a game of bullpen which was being held by Gene Primm, tennis pro at the Elinor Village Racquet Club in Ormond Beach/Daytona Beach Florida. I received a small trophy and it was love at first sight. Gene had a personality that made me want to play the game so I spent every free minute at the courts. He had smooth, effortless strokes that would become my role model and he epitomized fun and enthusiasm for the game. Elinor Village was a beautiful tennis club right off the ocean and it was a hot bed of tennis. Players came from all over the US and Canada to vacation in the area. Most of them played at Elinor Village because it had beautiful Har-Tru courts, a multitude of good players and you could always find a game. Many were famous/ranked adult and Jr. tennis players, who were kind enough to help kids with their tennis game. It was a hangout for Jr.'s and Adults and a fun environment. The environment of that club would develop many good tournament level Jr.'s who would go on to play high school and college tennis. I played for Seabreeze H.S., the best team in Northern Florida in the 60s. While playing high school tennis, I had the opportunity to travel to Los Angeles, California with my Dad. While there, I went to the

Beverly Hills municipal courts to play tennis. I met Vic Braden and joined in his fun tennis clinics. His philosophy of "laugh and win" would affect my game and life. He was the most passionate person that I had ever met. He was flowing with enthusiasm. He taught that tennis is more than a winning/losing situation. His teachings would remotely affect my tennis game as a teenager but would later affect my teaching of the game for my entire career.

My junior year of high school, I played the Southern Circuit (Jr. tennis tournaments in Florida, Alabama, Georgia and South Carolina). During the tour, I stayed in the house of a very benevolent tennis enthusiast, Dr. R. Walter (Whirlwind) Johnson, MD. and tennis coach. He was known as the Godfather of black tennis. During the summer, he opened his Virginia home (a kind of tennis commune) to tennis players. My doubles partner, whom I was traveling with, knew Dr. Johnson and he offered to let us stay in his home and practice tennis on his courts. He coached and was influential in the lives of Althea Gibson and Arthur Ashe. He loved talking tennis and gave written tennis quizzes. His focus was respect, sportsmanship and "no cheating, ever." He had a passionate relationship with the game of tennis.

I attended Austin Peay State University in Clarksville, Tennessee on a full ride tennis scholarship. My game and information would be affected by my two majors—Psychology and Philosophy. Polar opposites. Psychology is inside the mind—the source of all problems and Philosophy is the opening of the mind, the answer to all problems. The psychological influence was that of Gestalt theory, (the whole is greater than the sum of its parts and when you separate the parts from the whole, the outcome is struggle and resistance). Philosophy would open my mind and I became very interested in Zen's focus on mindfulness and being in the moment. APSU offered a course in transcendental meditation where I learned to clear my mind by letting go of my thoughts. The basic truth of mediation was that I have thoughts but I am not my thoughts. This empty mind approach would not only affect my play but would have an effect on my personalized teaching philosophy later in tennis career. But the greatest impact of my college career was not tennis related. It was the pursuing and marrying of my wife Gayle. We have been married for 42 years. She is the love of my life and my inspiration. She is my sounding board, my greatest supporter and the mother of my twins, Courtney and Kellie.

After graduating college, my first professional job was in Minneapolis Minnesota. I was a pro at Oakdale Indoor Racquet Club and worked with Owen Kennedy. He was an Australian tennis pro who was very playful in everything he did. He had a great sense of humor and focused on having fun on the court—not only while playing but also while teaching. His fun loving nature allowed people to progress naturally. I learned that tennis is a game first—play tennis, don't work tennis without having fun.

In the summers, I worked at St Cloud Country Club in St Cloud, Minnesota. It had an incredible tennis membership, not necessarily in numbers but in community awareness. Everyone supported the tennis program and was actively involved in assisting each other. It was the best that I felt about my teaching career. Everyone stood for the "good of all" and for the "good for the game of tennis". I loved the club and the community but unfortunately there were no indoor tennis clubs in St. Cloud so I was in search of a better job—my constant pursuit for stability.

I eventually ended up in Indianapolis, Indiana at Northeast Tennis Club. Joan Ramey, Master Professional from Ramey Tennis Camps/Schools was part owner of the club. We had been in contact verbally for a few years through mutual tennis students. However, we had never met. She wanted to cut down on her teaching schedule and asked me if I would take over the bulk of her lessons. Joan was definitely Ms. Fundamentals and was into precise execution of the tennis strokes. She was the first pro that I had taught with that was into custom fitting the game to the student. She was a true tennis enthusiast and a tireless worker. During that time, I purchased a copy the *Inner Game of Tennis* by Timothy Gallaway. It was an eye-opening book. His philosophy was all technical instruction needed to be converted into awareness where the body and mind are working in harmony. I saw great value in the book but could not find a quick way to utilize the *Inner Game* approach in the traditional, "fix it" teaching system I had been conditioned to use. Gallaway's insights would, however, greatly impact my teaching philosophy later on. Business was booming at the club but several owners were involved in the operation. They could not agree on where the club should focus and it was put up for sale. Another area club purchased NETC and I was not a part of their future plans. Off Gayle and I go again, right before Thanksgiving, this time with twins in tow—Courtney, my son and Kellie my daughter, who were born in Indianapolis.

We decided to head homeward for the holidays and search for a new job. We headed back to Ormond Beach, Florida, my home town to spend some time with my family and decide where we were going from there. Joan Ramey had contacted a club in Chicago who needed a pro in January so I already had an interview booked. The warm climate in my hometown, would afford me the luxury of playing outdoors during the fall to practice and work on my game. I had several contacts there that played at my level. The beginning of December, I started to contact my old tennis friends. My first contact was Bill Farmer, a nationally ranked Sr. player and a friend from my childhood days at Elinor Village Racquet Club. He was playing at a club called Ormond Beach Racquet Club and we met several times and practiced on the Har-Tru courts. I had no intention of staying in the Ormond Beach area but destiny was about to take over. On the morning of Christmas Eve, I received a phone call from Bill Farmer. He asked me to meet him for breakfast. He said he had something that he needed to talk to me about. He had been hired as the Tennis Director of Ormond Beach Racquet Club and asked me if I would consider taking the head pro job. After talking to Gayle, I decided to accept the position. Within a few months, Gayle was offered the bookkeeping job and we were a three-person team. Bill Farmer was an excellent player and a very religious man; a man of great faith. He always turned his game over to a higher source and often played inspired tennis. During my teaching there, I had a High School player whom I would accompany to the nationals in Burlingame, California. She would continue my desire for finding a better way. After observing me teach another junior player, she came to me and said, "I just observed you giving a lesson to someone who is not near my caliber and it seems that you gave her the same lesson as me. I don't understand." Those words would resonate within me and haunt me forever. I knew the answer was "tennis fundamentals are tennis fundamentals" and they are the same for everyone, regardless of level. But the unending question was still there—are they really the same for everyone? Am I teaching the game of tennis or am I teaching the person or am I teaching both? I had always adjusted the shots, feeds and drills based on the skills of the student but was I missing something?

After four years at the club, the owner became ill and decided to sell it. Because it was attached to the Ormond Hotel and the Casements, the former home of John D. Rockefeller, there was some clause in the agreement that the city had first right to the purchase of the facility. The city exercised that right and wanted to, at the time, turn it into a fire station. I attempted to lease the club, but the city wanted to have one of their recreational staff operate the facility. We had a couple of months left before the city took over and was now looking for another job.

One of my students was a member of a club in New York and she spent the summers there and the winters in Florida. She came to the club early one morning and said, "Here is a ticket to New York. The club where I play in the summer is looking for a new tennis pro. Gayle needs to reschedule your lessons because you fly out at one o'clock. Go home and pack and I will take you to the airport."

I flew in for the interview and they offered me the job on the spot. Look out Big Apple, here we come. We moved to New York within the next two weeks. I would teach in the summers at Scarsdale Golf Club but I needed to find a position indoors for the winter. My life was about to throw me a curveball. The tennis chairman at Scarsdale, had friends who were very active in an indoor tennis club in Hastings on the Hudson.

They set up an interview for me. I was about to encounter a tennis genius and his name was Gerry Alleyne. Gerry offered me the job at Hudson Valley and we would become great friends. We had many discussions about the game. He loved to talk about tennis, as did I. I immersed myself in his tennis wisdom and would spend hours absorbing his tennis savvy and taking hundreds of pages of notes after every encounter. Gerry had put together a technical, tactical progression from beginner to world-class level. This is it—the final answer, now I have everything that I have been searching for my entire tennis career. His conception-based teaching style seemed to blend perfectly with my mechanical upbringing; but a funny thing happened on the way to tennis enlightenment. I suddenly lost my Authentic self and my personal feel. I was no longer Bill Lefko—I became a Gerry clone. The more I overhauled my game, the worse I became. My tennis skills became so bad that I practically felt like a beginner on the court and my mind full of years of tennis knowledge could not deal with it. My game hit rock bottom; so where do I go from here? In spite of the fact that my game was in utter chaos this had nothing to do with Gerry, himself. I had always thought that knowledge was power and the final answer. I found out it wasn't. I had seized to function because Gerry's knowledge became more important than my personal feel. I greatly valued his information and approach but my breakdown occurred because I tried to totally reengineer my game instead of adapting it to my personal feel. This was a great learning experience for me and was one of the catalysts that would lead me to my personal teaching method—Authentic Tennis.

While in New York, I was offered a job in West Palm Beach, Florida by the former General Manager from Scarsdale Golf Club. We worked in the area over the next nine years and I continued to reconnect with my old game while infusing the newfound information into my game. My former student, friend and now co-author, Daniel Baird moved to the area. He, too, was passionate about the game of tennis. We practiced for hours together, working on our games. Daniel and I worked together, frequently, from the time I spent in West Palm Beach right up to present day, 25 years. We spent thousands of hours discussing a fundamental approach to teaching and learning the game. We were on a path of working from a more meditative focused state. As we spent hours on the court together, while I was looking for my feel by thinking about all the concepts that Gerry and I had worked on, Daniels gift began to take shape. Daniel realized that feel could not be captured through mechanics or thinking about the stroke. The more attached I was to form, the less I could feel; and the less I could feel the less I would be able to relax and feel the swing. I would often snap at Daniel "what do you mean don't be attached to my swing"? My past mechanical programming and my persistent over analysis was clearly the reason for my stroke paralysis. Little did I realize at the time that our vision for an Authentic philosophy was beginning to take shape. As our friendship continued to grow and evolve through the years, Daniel would always say that the known stroke form cannot know the unknown feel of it and that no two strokes could ever be exactly the same. This present moment realization would become a cornerstone of my development of Authentic Tennis. Even with Daniel's help and guidance I would continue to spend many frustrating hours on the tennis court.

I continued to feel like a Gerry clone. My personal game was getting better but my teaching skills were in a blunder. I did not feel comfortable in my teaching skin. The club where I taught was all Sr. Citizens and there were no Jr. players. I began to feel that I needed a change. I felt that if I needed get into a more natural and beautiful serene environment. I needed a peaceful club with a kid's program. I set my sights for North Carolina because I had played tournaments there as a Jr.

I found a job in Carolina and continued to experiment with my tennis knowledge. Daniel would continue to visit and we would spend hours brain storming about simplifying our teaching methods and creating a better world. I continued to struggle with tennis—I could not put the pieces together—knowledge was my security blanket and why was it not working? I was burned out mentally and felt like I might be coming to the end of the line with teaching tennis. None of the information that I had found satisfied my quest. Oh, I was still teaching, but I did not leave the courts feeling good. I did not realize it at the time but pain would become my catalyst for change. It seemed like it was time to lay my tennis racquets to rest. Where had my passion for the game taken me? Where did my quest for knowledge lead me? Where has my dedication and endless hour on the court led me? I went from the know, to the know nothing. I was about to lose my mind and come to my senses.

My wife's parents were not doing well health wise and we decided to pack up the tennis life and move back to Kentucky. I did not have a job. I had given up on tennis as a career even though I was still passionate about the game itself. I started to apply for UPS jobs, psychology jobs, and anything that was available to get me out of the tennis rat race. I hardly touched a tennis racquet for several months. Tennis never provided stability, so maybe I am in the wrong profession. We were here for nine months and I had given up on tennis but it had not given up on me. Then, a funny thing happened. The Hopkinsville Country Club tennis pro, who had worked there for years during the summer, decided to take a year round job with the school system. He recommended me for the job and I took it out of desperation. I knew that if I returned to my old way that I would literally lose my mind and totally burn out again. Darkness often precedes the light and breakdowns often come before breakthroughs.

I had only planned to teach there for the summer while continuing to search for a new profession. I knew that I would have to build the tennis program from scratch because the club had very few active tennis players. As I began pulling people out of the pool and putting tennis racquets in their hand, I recognized that there was potential in this little club. Word of mouth spread and people starting coming to the tennis courts. My son, Courtney had been by my side from the first day and his charismatic, natural enthusiastic personality was a natural fit. He loves people and is a natural leader. He has an uncanny way of making people feel good about who they are as individuals. He sacrificed a lot to help me regain my enthusiasm and love for the game. We are still working together as a Father and Son team and we have both grown as a result of this relationship. I am indebted to him and love him from the bottom of my heart. As we worked endless hours to rebuild the tennis program, I decided that I was going to return to the love that I felt for the game when I was a kid. I would return to the mind of the beginner. I realized tennis was a game that needed to be developed from the inside out. The genius lies within each individual's personal feel. Simply by guiding their awareness, they would naturally develop the tennis skills. I focused on fun with my students as well as myself. Daniel would continue to visit several times a year and we relentlessly brain stormed to refine a philosophy for learning and teaching the game. This philosophy would reenergize our approach to teaching tennis and revive my teaching career. I, along with my son, Courtney, created a tennis boom in Hopkinsville, Kentucky and through that reconnection with the fun and love of the game, I found Authentic Tennis.

You can see from the brief overview of my personal story that tennis is my destiny and that the unique life paths that I have crossed were not by coincidence but were meant to be. They were by design and would provide perspective and inspiration to my search for finding the missing link. That link is feel is the foundation of mastery in tennis and all things in life.

1 AUTHENTIC APPROACH:
AWAKEN YOUR TENNIS GENIUS

THERE ARE TWO DISTINCTLY different paths that you could choose to travel on your journey to discover your personal best tennis swing. This is a tale of two different approaches, each having their own unique story, each with a different beginning and ending. One path begins at the lost origins of the tennis swing and guides you through a natural order. This path is called Authentic Tennis. The other path begins with an imitated technical model of the tennis swing and takes you through a replicating sequence. This path is called the mechanical method.

The path of Authentic Tennis uses a holistic feel based approach to tennis. This Authentic approach makes the feel of the swing primary, while the mechanical method tends to make body mechanics primary. The mechanical method to the tennis swing emphasizes the form of the swing over the feel of the swing. "Feel" is something that cannot be seen. Each person's "feel" is completely unique and personal and the mechanical method does not recognize its immeasurable value. For Authentic Tennis, "feel" is its cornerstone and serves as the foundation of swing mastery. "Feel" is an individual process that makes it un-teachable through a mechanical system that separates the mind from the body. However, through mindfulness and awareness centered consciousness "feel" becomes an integrating process that allows for natural mind/body connection.

The Authentic approach to the tennis swing believes in the unlimited potential of each individual to access their God given talents. Authentic Tennis accesses one's natural state of learning, the mind of the beginner that can be observed in babies and very young children. This "empty mind" observer state of consciousness works from inside out and focuses on the uniqueness of each moment. The inside-out path to the tennis swing arises from a human being's innate unconditioned potential and shows up in the world of form. The mechanical or outside-in path to the tennis swing works off conditioned outside form through memory and programming and thereby limits human potential. It treats the human being like a computerized robot or machine. Authentic Tennis realizes that the human being has a soul and consciousness and that our ability to be aware and to feel, (sense), is our greatest gift.

Cause and effect is the underlying principle in our ability to understand the world of form, as is the case for the tennis swing. In Authentic Tennis the swing form is an effect of the basic nature of the swing and the swing feel. The mechanical method tends to see effects, what one can see in the swing, and treat those effects as causal, similar to building more prisons to stop crime or manufacturing more drugs to cure disease. These effects are all symptoms of the real cause. The mechanical method or the outside-in path, band aids problems in the tennis swing without getting to the root cause or the source of the problem. The problem's source lies within our very consciousness. Consciousness is the source to the feel connection in all our actions. There are numerous possible swing problems, but only one solution. The solution to deal with a swing problem or any other problem for that matter is to engage it at its causal level or the level of feel. Feel is not part of the visible world or the world of form. When a swing problem is engaged from the inside or feels level, it transforms the swing rather than just modifying it from the outside, which are the symptoms of the problem, not the cause.

Authentic Tennis realizes and applies this core principle to the tennis swing; anything visible in the stroke is an effect. Conventional thought on tennis, views anything visible as the cause. For example, a tennis instructor may see you stop your racquet on contact with the tennis ball and recommend that you follow through next time. However, both the racquet coming to a stop and the lack of follow through are symptoms of the problem and not the problem itself. The mechanical method constantly tries to solve the problem from the same level of understanding (the level of form), created it in the first place. The inability to guide awareness to the invisible cause of the problem (lack of feel), creates resistance and tension in the swing. The Authentic approach will use the empty mind qualities of observation, awareness and mindfulness to differentiate between cause and effect.

The Authentic approach to the tennis swing aligns to the creative processes as observed in nature. Nature goes through a creative process where all living things, trees, flowers, animals, etc., originate from the unseen and take form, then expand, contract and die. The only constant in nature is change. In nature everything changes from moment to moment. Applying this process to the Authentic swing allows the swing to follow a natural order. The tennis swing is literally born from the unseen, it expands, contracts, and then it dies or finishes. At that moment it is time to create a new swing. No two swings can ever be exactly the same, just as in signing your name; no two signatures are exactly the same. As in nature, the unseen initiates the creative processes, so too, does it initiate the creative process of the tennis swing. When one approaches the tennis swing in terms of something to be programmed or conditioned, it becomes the unnatural mechanical method. By attempting to reproduce or program a tennis swing, it makes the swinging action non-adaptive and inflexible to change. The Authentic approach to tennis sees every swing as something to be created anew, making it adaptable and flexible to the uniqueness of the moment. The simplicity and truth inherent in the Authentic approach will have profound transformational benefits, for all levels of play from beginner to world class.

So, please join us on a journey to create your Authentic Tennis swing by awakening your tennis genius inside. Authentic Tennis will chart a path for you to unlock your unlimited potential and to see the infinite possibilities. Hold on to your racquet and get ready for the ride of your life!

2 THE FIVE ESSENTIAL TENNIS STROKES: THE ORIGIN, FOUNDATION, AND EVOLUTION OF THE TENNIS SWING

NOW THAT YOU RECOGNIZE the difference between the mechanical method and the path of Authentic Tennis it is time to prepare for your journey to find your custom fit tennis swing. Regardless of the path you choose, Authentic Tennis welcomes you to this fun adventure.

If you have chosen Authentic Tennis as your path, you will begin your journey at the source or origins of the tennis swing. If you have chosen the mechanical method as your path you will begin your journey by analyzing and trying to imitate the perfect tennis swing model.

The game of tennis has been played in many forms for centuries. It came to the forefront in France in the 14th century but historians have traced it back to the ancient Greeks and Romans. In these early days, tennis was played without a racquet, over a rope and with the open hand—no racquet. It was known in France as, *Jeu De Paume*, game of the hand. It is clear from the early days that hand feel was primary to the swing and the game.

The game of tennis was originally played without any tennis instructions. As the game progressed or evolved, crude racquets were introduced and the ball was gradually improved upon. Through time and as technology advanced, tennis became more popular and the number of players steadily increased. Soon tennis instructors began to pop up to meet the demand of the games wide spread popularity. Recognize that the game existed prior to the tennis instructor. Personal feel came before and instructional "how-to" approach.

Tennis took a giant leap forward when, in the late 1800s an English man by the name of Major Walter Wingfield, brought the game to England. He created a set of standardized tennis rules and made it an outdoor grass court sport, the same surface that Wimbledon is played on today.

There are many variables that make tennis an interesting and challenging sport. The tennis court itself, is a constant, its dimensions never change. The tennis court is a rectangle; 78feet long by 36 feet wide for doubles and 78 feet long by 27 feet wide for singles. It has a net that is three feet high in the middle and three feet six inches on the sides.

Even though the tennis court is a constant, it is your personal feel that connects you to both the swing and the game. Tennis is an open skill, like driving a car where the conditions of play are constantly changing. Your personal feel is constantly adapting to the changing environment and is primary to that which connects you to the court, the game, and the swing. There is a tendency in the tennis world to put form over feel and to see the form of the swing and the dimensions of the court as more important than your personal feel. While the objective in tennis is to put the ball over the net and into the court, success is really the result of personal swing feel. Don't let the court act as a barrier, making you afraid to miss. Literally, a player can become court bound, which can create an uneasy tension in the swing. "I must not miss the court or hit the ball into the net" can be a recipe for tight muscles and restricting swing flow. This same type of experience can occur when preparing to stroke the tennis ball. The player can treat the ball as a threat. "I must not miss the ball" can result in tension in the swing. The player becomes ball bound, afraid to swing freely through the ball. Always keep a relaxed swing feel as your number one priority.

The Five Basic Tennis Strokes

Before you learn the five basic tennis strokes you will need to discover the difference between stroking and hitting a ball. **Stroking** a tennis ball originates from the swing's hand feel, the hands being the pathway of feel. In tennis, the racquet head is an extension of the hand, allowing for a sweeping-like natural movement through the ball. Stroking a tennis ball with the racquet implies a kind of touch or caressing feeling. It builds momentum gradually and transfers energy through the ball, smoothly and effortlessly. Hitting a tennis ball is not the same as stroking it. **Hitting** can be a byproduct of the mechanical method. Hitting implies using excessive effort in a quick, forceful, and abrupt action and lacks the feel of the racquet head sweeping through the ball.

The tennis racquet is an instrument with strings much like a guitar. To play the guitar you need to feel the strings. Feeling the ball on the strings of a tennis racquet is the essence of feeling the stroke. Hitting the ball with excessive effort and abruptness produces tension which short-circuits the ability to make a relaxed swing. When it comes to stroking the tennis ball, muscle tension and tightness is public enemy No. 1.

While the tennis strokes can be taught in many different ways, all possible tennis shots come off of the five basic strokes. These five basic strokes are the starting point for learning the game and will provide the foundation for advancement of all strokes. All swinging games depend on stroke efficiency through personal feel. The five basic tennis strokes are the forehand volley, the backhand volley, the forehand ground stroke, the backhand ground stroke and the serve. The volley is played out of the air and feels like a catching motion. It does not have a lot of backswing or forward movement. The forehand ground stroke is a side arm motion similar to the feel of skipping a rock across water. The one handed backhand ground stroke is a side arm motion, similar to throwing a Frisbee. For the two handed backhand the left hand is dominant like a left handed forehand. This would be reversed for left handed players. The serve is the stroke that initiates play and begins all points. It is an upward throwing motion and feels like you are throwing your racquet from the baseline over the net into the opposite side of the court.

The mechanical method of teaching the five basic tennis strokes is that they are unnatural actions and therefore the strokes are counter intuitive and can not be naturally developed. By seeing these five basic tennis strokes as counter intuitive, they address the swing from a mechanical point of view. The mechanical method puts the swing together in step-by-step sequential fashion using memory to program the body. This method divorces the feel of the swing from the stroke by breaking it down into parts. It loses the integrated feel of the swing as a whole.

The Three Feel Familiar Athletic Actions

Authentic Tennis advocates that the tennis swing is both natural and intuitive. The five basic tennis strokes work off of the foundation of the three feel familiar athletic actions. These three feel familiar athletic actions are catching (volley motion), side arm throw (ground strokes), and upward throwing motion (the serve). There are many other physical feel familiar actions that are related and transferable to the five basic tennis strokes. These include, but are not limited to, throwing a javelin (the serve), throwing a Frisbee (the one handed backhand), throwing a sack of potatoes (two handed backhand), skipping a rock (the forehand), catching balls at different heights (forehand volley), Karate back fist (one handed back hand volley). The feel familiar action of hammering a nail, gives you an excellent feel reference for the racquet head's application to the ball for all strokes. The point of feel action is the hammer head meeting the nail or the strings of the racquet head meeting the ball. Many of the three feel familiar core athletic actions can be observed in other games, like golf and baseball, which produce swinging action.

Authentic Tennis realizes that the five basic tennis strokes can be learned more naturally and intuitively, just as one learns to crawl, walk, run, swim, or ride a bike. The body's wisdom in a feeling state is more powerful than learning through any informational system. If the information is in the head but is not experienced by the body, the action lacks feel. Knowing does not equal doing when it comes to physical action. "Doing" always precedes "understanding." A Chinese proverb illustrates this point beautifully, "I hear I forget, I see I remember, I do I understand."

If you are a beginner or if you are an experienced player struggling with any of the five basic strokes, go out and experience the three feel familiar core athletic swinging actions. Get reacquainted with your personal hand feel, without a racquet. Simplify and return to the natural origins of the tennis swing with the exercises below. The beauty of these natural feel-based exercises, is that they can be done anywhere where a ball will bounce—a patio, driveway or even on a hardwood floor.

For the forehand or two handed backhand volley (left handed forehand), practice a patty-cake type catching motion by tossing a ball up at different heights, matching up the palm of your right or left hand with the height of the ball and catching it. Then practice using that catching, patty-cake type motion to propel (push), the ball forward with the palm of the suitable hand. This will give you the flat hand feel for the forehand or two handed backhand volley.

For the one handed backhand volley, imagine propelling the ball forward with the back of your hand.

For the forehand ground stroke, experience the feeling of throwing the ball forward with a side arm throwing motion. Then practice using your side arm motion to propel (push), the ball forward with the palm of your hand. This will give you the flat hand feel for the forehand ground stroke.

For the one handed backhand, experience the feel of tossing a ball forward with a side arm motion like throwing a Frisbee. We do not recommend propelling with the backside of your hand for either the one handed backhand volley or ground stroke.

For the two handed backhand (it is like a left handed forehand), experience the feeling of throwing the ball forward using a side arm throwing motion with your left hand. Then experience the feel of propelling (pushing), the ball forward with the palm of your left hand.

For the serve, experience the feel of throwing a ball up high in the air and forward. Imagine throwing a ball up on the roof of your house. This will give the feel for the upward throwing motion used on the serve. Then practice propelling (pushing) the ball forward with your hand using the upward throwing motion. These hand feel exercises are simple but fundamental to the feel of the strokes, regardless of ability level. They will benefit all levels of players and are not just for beginners.

As you can see, you don't need to be a rocket scientist to stroke a tennis ball. Don't let yourself get absorbed in the details of how the tennis swing works. If you start to see the tennis swing as overly difficult and something that requires a lot of thought, it can lead to trying too hard to do it right and not to do it wrong. This type of mental duality can divide attention and condition resistance and tension in the swinging action.

The Authentic Tennis invitation is to focus on what you are feeling in your swing at all times, and that will allow your "personal best" swing to find you. If this seems too simplistic for you, recognize that there are really only two types of tennis games being played, the world-class game and everybody else at less than world-class level. The world-class game is like looking at the peak of the mountain. The world-class player has trained for hours and years to reach the top of that mountain peak but he/she, too, had to have a starting point.

As a result of viewing the finished product of a world-class swing and game, the foundation for the tennis stroke has become obscured. Authentic Tennis begins from the game's original foundation and what is most natural to the tennis stroke. Authentic Tennis starts as a game of the hand, "jeu de paume," just as it did in France in the 1400s and guides you through the metamorphosis process to find your Authentic swing and be at your personal best. To climb to the top of your personal mountain, you need a starting point, which will allow you to progress through the many levels of the game. Your swing and game will evolve naturally on your journey while you are having fun, learning and playing the game.

The Racquet Head is Primary

In stroking a tennis ball over the net, the primary message delivered to the ball is applied by the racquet head, which as mentioned earlier, is an extension of the hand. Authentic Tennis will continually emphasize the racquet head is primary and the body is secondary to the stroking action of a tennis swing. The mechanical method for manufacturing the tennis stroke tends to indicate that the body is primary or causal and the racquet head and relaxed swing is secondary or an effect of the body. It sees the body as moving the swing rather than seeing the swing as moving the body.

When the body is viewed as moving the tennis swing, this can lead to a disconnection between the feel of the swing and the racquet head's application to the ball. The end result is a muscled or forced stroke with the body doing too much or too little.

When the racquet head is viewed as primary throughout the swinging action, it will orchestrate the body's motion, allowing the body to respond effortlessly to the rhythm and movement of the swing and racquet head.

When the racquet head and swing are seen as primary, the body will both support and work in harmony with the swinging action. The sense of what the racquet head is doing puts the mind and the body on the same page so that the body will not overpower the swing or get too far ahead of the swinging action. A relaxed swinging action with the racquet head sweeping through the ball is the essence of an Authentic swing.

Flat is Fundamental

Returning to the origin of the game of tennis, the hand and specifically the palm of the hand (flat hand) is fundamental to the relationship to the racquet head. Authentic Tennis suggests learning the game of tennis through a flat hand feel. However, there is no such thing as a totally flat swing or shot. Due to the upward lifting action of the tennis swing to send the ball over the net, there is naturally a slight amount of topspin, where the top of the ball rotates forward.

Flat creates a foundational and starting point for the swing, as all spin variations come off of a nearly flat hand. Flat is the center between the racquet face coming off of the ball, either by coming over top of it (topspin) or underneath it (slice or under spin). Once the feel for flat has become feel familiar, spin variations will come easily. Learning spin first, will most likely hinder your ability to feel the benefits of flat. Flat is the feel foundation for drive force. While styles of play of the game come and go, flat ball striking is timeless and never goes out of style. What does the flat hand and nearly flat racquet face allow you to feel that is foundational to the swing?

The Timeless Technical Benefits of Flat

1. Flat allows you to feel compression, where the ball sinks into the string bed. This is known as the trampoline effect. The

trampoline effect creates a sense or feeling of both absorbing (catching the ball on the strings) and propelling (carrying the ball forward and off the strings).

2. Flat allows you to feel a sense of the racquet head being directly behind the ball. This ability to stroke the ball straight, is fundamental to both swing timing and developing consistency. Timing is the player's connection between the hand, the racquet head, the ball and the target. It depends on the player's personal feel. As far as timing is concerned, if you are too early or too late, you will end up spraying or deflecting the ball either to the right or to the left as compared to the hook or shank in golf. Flat hand feel establishes timing and can serve as a foundation for recognizing errors.

3. Flat allows you to feel the racquet head and hand staying behind the ball much longer than spin. This action for stroking through the ball allows for more feel between the hand/racquet head as connected to the target. Topspin, with its greater net clearance is more forgiving for keeping the ball in the court. However, it does not establish the flat hand feel for drive force or the racquet head sweeping through the ball.

4. Flat allows you to feel the most fundamental relationship of the tennis stroke, which is the hand and racquet head's relationship to the ball. Flat or palm feel is the easiest and most feel familiar hand position to sense the ball on the strings.

5.   Flat allows you to feel a more "on center" solid contact, resulting in fewer miss-hits of the ball. Authentic Tennis is not

suggesting that spin is not valuable to an advanced game. We are suggesting flat serves as the source of feel for all strokes. Be aware that flat does not mean playing every stroke with maximum force or hitting net skimmers; it is simply a reference for the point of contact between the racquet head and the ball. From the baseline, a nearly flat ground stroke will clear the net by an average of one to two feet. As you move forward in the court, the height of the ground stroke will be slightly lowered.

To acquire a flat hand feel, start by looking at the way you hold the handle of the racquet, known as your grip. There is no right or wrong way to hold the racquet. Hand grips, over time, are usually custom fit to personal feel. Many #1 ranked players in the world have used a variety of forehand grips successfully, including the eastern, composite, continental, semi-western and western grips. There are grip variations on all the other strokes, as well. Authentic Tennis suggests as a starting point, the eastern or shake hands grip. Use the eastern grip for all strokes that utilize the palm of the hand. These include the forehand volley, the forehand ground stroke, the two handed backhand (top hand only) and the serve. To find the eastern grip, for either right or left hand, place your hand flat on the racquet face, and then slide your hand down until you can shake hands with the grip. For the one backhand volley and ground strokes, Authentic Tennis suggests an eastern backhand grip where the palm of the hand is more on top of the racquet rather than behind the handle. The eastern backhand grip gives the best feel for a firm but flexible wrist and solid contact. To find the eastern backhand grip, take your eastern forehand grip and turn your hand counter clock wise if right handed and clockwise if left handed. Allow the hand to sit comfortably on top of the grip with the racquet head remaining flat or square. Spreading your fingers slightly for all grips, may give you a better feel. Experiment, it is your personal feel.

Authentic Tennis is not suggesting these grips are the only possible grips to stroke a tennis ball effectively. We simply are using these grips as optimal, for creating a feel foundation for flat with its previously mentioned benefits. Furthermore, it is extremely helpful, regardless of ability level, to go back to these grips to transform a stroke lacking in hand feel.

You are now ready to get your racquet and go to the tennis court. Apply the flat hand feel while using the eastern grip to the three feel familiar athletic actions. Start with the catching action of the volley. Get fairly close to the net. Toss some balls up approximately at chest level. Using your eastern, shake hands grip, volley the balls over the net. Feel the sensation of absorbing the ball on the strings and propelling it forward. Experience the feel of the racquet being an extension of the hand. Use your left hand if you have a two handed backhand volley. Reverse the process if you are a left-handed player. Please note that the volley uses a slightly downward action on balls above the level of the net. For balls shoulder height and higher, the racquet face will need to be slightly closed. For balls below the level of the net, the racquet face will be somewhat open. Always focus on matching the racquet head up with the ball.

Now, take your eastern backhand grip for the one handed backhand volley, and follow the exercise above. Feel the racquet head flat, solid and behind the ball on contact. Notice your strings facing straight ahead.

We are aware that many players are taught to volley with under spin, coming down on the ball with a slightly open face. We are suggesting that developing a flat hand feel and solid contact behind and through the ball will be the basis of mastering all variations of spin on all strokes within your personal feel.

Next, find your eastern forehand grip. Toss some balls up around waist level. Let the ball bounce and use the side arm throwing motion to stroke the ball over the net. Playing the ball at waist level at the top of the bounce is the most natural position for learning a flat ground stroke. Do the same with your top hand if you have a two handed backhand. Get the sense of the flat hand feel and solid contact on the ball, while taking a relaxed swing.

For the one handed backhand use your eastern backhand grip and apply the Frisbee type throwing action and stroke some balls over the net. Feel the sense of a long relaxed smooth swing with solid contact.

For the serve, use the eastern forehand grip and toss the ball up, slightly higher than your reach. Throw the racquet head up to the ball making contact at the highest point that you can stretch. Get the feeling of throwing the racquet up and out toward the service boxes while keeping the upward throwing motion smooth and relaxed. Authentic Tennis realizes that the serve can be taught using other grips. As with the other strokes, we suggest that flat hand feel, solid contact and stroking through the ball is the foundation for all other stroking actions.

With all the tennis exercises do not attempt to kill the ball. Tennis is a stroking game. None of the strokes require excessive effort. Keep all strokes relaxed, smooth and solid.

The Natural Evolution of the Swing

The tennis strokes evolve naturally when the strokes are aligned to the creative process, where feel is primary and form is secondary. Feel familiarity expands through a natural progression, just like a small seed grows into a giant tree. By observing nature you will recognize the differences between natural evolution and mechanical evolution. Likewise, by observing tennis strokes you will begin to recognize the differences between a mechanical swing and a natural swing or stroke. What are some of the observable qualities seen in nature that are transferable to the tennis swing?

1. Nature creates. It goes through a creative process where living things are born, expand, contract, and die.
2. Nature is effortless. There is no trying in nature, just being and responding to what is.
3. Nature is constantly changing. Change is the only constant in the universe.
4. Nature adapts. It is continually readjusting itself to meet external challenges.

5. Nature is deliberate. It is always in the present. It possesses the quality of surrendered action, the action of non-resistance.

6. Nature responds to the cause. It responds to that which cannot be seen.

7. Nature balances itself through a process of transformation.

8. Nature follows a natural order. Tides roll in and out, the sun rises and sets and seasons come and go.

9. Nature is timeless. It is a creative process without a beginning or end.

What are some of the observable techniques seen in machines that are utilized to teach the tennis strokes when using the mechanical method?

1. Machines are manufactured, part-by-part and step-by-step, through assembly lines. There are no creative possibilities with a machine.

2. Machines are built through a work of effort. There is no feel present within them, therefore they cannot respond to what is, only react to a program.

3. Machines are stagnant. They do not change and evolve; they only break down and deteriorate.

4. Machines are not conscious. They possess none of the feel qualities of consciousness.

5. Machines are a result of being manufactured. They cannot respond to the unseen cause or real source.

6. Machines are an artificial product, therefore they cannot be transformed.

7. Machines follow a programmed order, which is separate from the natural world and natural processes.

8. Machines cannot evolve through the creative process. They require new technology in order to improve, a kind of mechanical evolution.

9. Machines are on a time table and become obsolete. New mechanical technology is constantly updating or changing machines.

Through observing the differences between nature and machine it becomes evident that nature evolves through awareness and consciousness, which is natural human state. **You are not a machine!** Your tennis swing will evolve most effectively, by connecting to your natural state, where feel and creativity are present. By being present or deliberate, adaptive, balanced, effortless, and creative, your tennis strokes will evolve naturally just as nature does.

3 CREATING SWING FEEL:
THE UNNOTICED PATH TO MASTERY

SO FAR ON YOUR Authentic adventure to find your inherent, natural tennis swing, you have noticed the difference between the Authentic path and the mechanical method. You have prepared yourself for your journey by rediscovering the origins of your swing. Now pack your backpack with the three core athletic actions that serve as a compass for the five basic strokes. Place your racquet in your bag and realize that the racquet head is an extension of your flat hand feel. As you begin your personally selected journey down tennis lane, allow your tennis swing to naturally evolve.

If you have your bags packed to walk the path of the mechanical method, bring a book with the latest scientific analysis of the tennis swing. Make sure you bring your cell phone so you can call your tennis instructor and watch your minutes; it could become a costly trip. Bring along a battery powered DVD player to watch tapes on the perfect tennis swing model they want you to copy. Good luck!

Since your destiny to your Authentic swing is still unclear you may need some further assistance to navigate the terrain. Its time to awaken your internal compass of feel and allow the aware feel principles, explored in this chapter, to point the way and illuminate your path to your natural swing. If you are using the mechanical method you need to bring along your programmed memory containing the thousands of details and tips on how the swing works.

Feel arises naturally when you recognize that feel is your natural state and that programmed memory is a conditioned state. In the mechanical method, the #1 tool to understanding the tennis swing is memory. The tennis player tries to remember all the parts that make up the tennis swing and then hope they show up. "Feel" is unknown and cannot be captured by programmed memory, which is the known. You can feel the swing but you can never really know it. The true cause of the physical universe will always remain unknown. Whether or not you believe this is true you will discover that it is the optimal point of view for creating feel. The memory program wants to know the swing, possess it, and control it. Mission impossible! Understanding the tennis swing is far too complicated of a process to be consciously controlled by that which you have previously learned. Feel arises from the unknown; it cannot be possessed or controlled. In applying this realization to the tennis swing, feel becomes present when everything you encounter on your path to finding your swing, is viewed as the known (an effect), and not the cause.

Feel is the creative process itself and no process can be known. Process is formless and cannot be dissected or separated by the known, which only deals with form or what can be seen. The known (form) can never know the unknown (process). This incredible gift of feel is obscured through focusing on the known, which blocks your personal access to feel. The creative process moves from the unknown to the known and from feel to form.

The mechanical method only moves from what is known about the swing to a quest for more knowledge. It under values and disconnects the feel, which is the underlying foundation of swing mastery. Feel is invisible and because it is unseen it is treated as secondary or a byproduct of the mechanical method. To put it another way, the outside or form will create the inside or feel. However, this is simply just another way the mechanical method tries to reverse the natural creative process. Within the creative process, change is the only constant. Programmed memory does not have a way to handle change, because the known (form), is always changing. The past memory program cannot keep up with this continuous change in the present. Feel can adapt to change because it is always present and only the now adapts to the now.

Unfortunately, the mechanical method does not allow the tennis player to reach their true potential. Your potential cannot be reached solely through a programmed memory instructional method. It is unnatural to learn physical actions, like the tennis swing, through an information based system. Most tennis players are unable to take programmed memory and convert it into personal feel as related to a physical action. The conventional belief is that you can learn through programmed memory and feel will show up as the form improves.

Have you ever seen a machine have a feel-based awareness for its actions? When a tennis player attempts to convert information (the known) into a feel (the unknown) for the tennis swing it usually gets lost in translation.

Before you can make a connection between the unknown feel of the swing and the known form of the swing, you need to become aware of the natural consequences of being in feel. Authentic Tennis refers to the natural outcomes of being in feel as the aware-feel principles. While feel is your natural state, most of us have lost track of feel by over using programmed memory to perform physical action. By noticing feel is not present in your physical actions, such as the tennis swing, the aware-feel principles will act as your friendly feel guides to take you back toward your natural feeling state. Creating an awareness of these principles will transform your tennis experience. Let these aware-feel principles be your friendly feel guides to light the way on your path to discovering your own unique tennis swing. Your internal navigational compass of feel will expand and create feel familiarity through these aware-feel principles. The aware-feel principles will guide you toward your full swing potential by bringing out and connecting you to your personal feel and allowing that feel to create and shape your Authentic swing. The aware-feel principles have no order of importance and are not meant to be over analyzed. These principles are noticeable in all physical actions throughout your daily life and within your daily tasks.

Aware-Feel Principles

1. When you are in feel, aligned to your Authentic swing, there is **no unnecessary tension** in the body, particularly in the shoulders, arms, and hands.

2. When you are in feel, aligned to your Authentic swing, there is **racquet head awareness**.

3. When you are aligned to your personal feel, your body and swing **match the energy to the task or target**. The body and racquet head neither does too much or too little. You only use as much energy as you can feel.

4. When you are in feel, there is a **line of energy awareness**, a connection between the ball and target through a line of energy.

5. When you are aligned to your Authentic swing, **a natural rhythm and timing awareness is present**. A feel connecting you to the ball, racquet, and target.

6. Authentic swing feel creates a **spatial awareness**. An awareness of the space between the body, racquet, and ball. You are in a personal comfort zone which is neither too far away or too close to the ball.

7. When you are in a feel based Authentic swing, there is a **time and distance awareness**. There is a feel for the amount of time available for the swing, as connected to the speed of the ball and your position on the court.

8. There is an **absorbing and propelling awareness**. An awareness and feel that connects the ball to the target through the length of the swing.

9. Authentic swing feel allows a feeling impression of the target through the mind's eye (an internal mental picture of the court). It creates **internal court dimension awareness**.

10. When you are in feel, aligned to your Authentic swing, there is a **visual, auditory, and kine-static awareness**. An awareness and feel that allows your sight, hearing, and sense of touch to work together.

These aware-feel principles point and illuminate the way to your Authentic Tennis swing. As you connect them to the three core athletic actions, along with your flat hand feel, you will expand your feel familiarity for the tennis swing. As your feel of any of the core athletic actions expand and align to the tennis swing, the action itself becomes more feel familiar through pattern recognition. Authentic Tennis realizes that the feeling process, which creates feel familiarity, is the foundation for all physical experience. Even a highly trained tennis player, who hasn't played in a long time, would find it challenging to keep the ball in the court and regain his/her natural rhythm, timing, and accuracy without regaining their feel familiarity. If the memory program were the key to regaining previous form they could just turn on the program, then presto, all the strokes would be back the way they were. The missing link is the unnoticed relationship between feel, that which is unknown, and familiar, that which is known. Feel familiarity is developed when physical actions are transformed by feel, into recognizable patterns. Notice the feel familiarity that is present in your daily personal physical actions, such as your arms swinging naturally as you are walking. Notice the point of action when riding a bike, using a fork to eat, brushing your teeth, pulling a door open, etc. When feel moves from the unknown into the known, feel familiarity is naturally created. When the familiar is divorced from feel that is when habit becomes part of the memory program. Habit is the familiar minus the feel. Habit is never present because it is a product of a conditioned past program. You could say that there is no such thing as a good habit, because habit has lost its connection to feel—the present.

Feel Familiarity

To gain further insight into the nature of feel familiarity, let's explore the differences between feel familiarity and programmed memory (habit). Notice the difference between intimacy (which is feel based) and information (which is programmed memory based). For example, compare the feel of being with your spouse, children, mother or father, to a casual relationship with a person that you hardly know. In the feel familiarity relationships, you relate to your loved ones through their presence and essence. Many hours of attention, care and connection has created a feel familiar relationship. In contrast, there is no feel familiar relationship with a relative stranger. Therefore, you relate to a casual relationship through a memorized program of impersonal acceptable responses; "Good Morning" or "How are you?" They are just greetings with no real personal feel. Feel familiarity taps into the higher realms of consciousness like intuitiveness, creativity, and observation. So, nurture your swing, with care and attention, as you would an intimate relationship. A simple acknowledgment, like in a casual relationship lacks nurturing qualities.

It is now time to have a more intimate relationship with your swing. Take your racquet to the tennis court and tap into your personal feel. You have already experienced the three core athletic actions. Now it is time to allow the aware-feel principles, your friendly feel guides, to expand your senses and guide the shaping of your Authentic swing through feel familiarity.

Using the eastern grips explore the ground strokes, the side arm throwing motions. Connect the side arm throwing motion to the aware-feel principles as you explore your forehand or backhand. Notice any unnecessary tension, particularly in the shoulder, arm, and hand. Stroke a few balls over the net, noticing if there is a line of energy connecting the racquet and the ball to your intended target.

Move inside the service line, close to the net and use the catching motion to explore the feel of your volley. Do you have a sense of absorbing and propelling the ball off the strings, a kind of catch and carry feeling? Notice if there is racquet head awareness based on flat hand feel.

Practice serving some balls over the net into the service boxes, using the upward overhand throwing action. Notice if you are matching the energy to the task. Notice if you are doing too much or too little and be aware of only using as much energy as you can feel.

Chapter Eight will give you many feel-based exercises to expand your feel familiarity in creating your Authentic swing.

All the aware feel principles apply to every stroke. As you notice your feel familiarity expanding, the human tendency to expect a certain result may creep in. The result may become more important than the process of creating the swing. Here is a secret, a valuable insight into Authentic wisdom. This will focus your attention on the process rather than the results—allow, do not try!

Allowing vs. Trying

Let's explore the feeling difference between allowing and trying. Trying is a byproduct of memory programming, whose motto is "if something is not working, try harder." **Trying** is the energy of resistance. Trying is judgmental by nature and it is a forced method. Trying creates a separation between you and what you are doing. Trying is connected to desire whose counterpart is resistance. Trying puts the programmed memory in a state of division between wanting to do something right and resisting doing something wrong. This constant tension within the programmed memory, conditioned by trying, creates a division between the body and mind and therefore, restricts your access to feel familiarity. Trying makes your tennis swing literally more mechanical and stiff. Trying, very often, is a reaction to doubt and doubt leads to the tendency to want to over control. Trying often utilizes excessive effort and excessive effort leads to physical tightness as the memory program imposes tension on the body. Tension short-circuits and neutralizes feel. In short, trying fails and is the programmed outcome of the mechanical method.

Allowing is a receptive quality that occurs naturally when the mind is not engaged in programmed memory or trying. Allowing is the energy of non-resistance. Allowing integrates and creates a mental space to feel what you are doing. Allowing is outside of any conditioned program and creates no desire or resistance to what is happening. Allowing embraces all possibilities, for example, making or missing, winning or losing, and uses them as feedback. Allowing is the optimal state to produce a holistic integrated response that occurs naturally when the mind and body are in harmony. Allowing accesses feel familiarity by not interfering with your unified state. Allowing moves your tennis swing into the creative process where you and the creative process join together. Allowing does not concern itself with doubt and there is simply a faith in the process. Allowing leads to relaxation in the body and creates effortlessness in the swing. In essence, allowing lets feel take the wheel and while the body come along for the ride. Allowing works! Welcome to the world of Authentic Tennis. Now, let's discover what shows up in the swing, the effects of the swinging action, what Authentic Tennis refers to as the fundamental swing properties.

4 THE BASIC NATURE OF THE SWING: THE FUNDAMENTAL SWING PROPERTIES

IF YOU HAVE BEEN on the journey to your Authentic natural swing, the path has been illuminated by the aware-feel principles, your "friendly feel guides." However, like any path traveled, you will experience challenges along the way. The way you meet these challenges will determine your final destination. If your journey is still along the path of the mechanical method, you have been carrying with you the latest tennis information goodies. You have been studying diligently and have been programming your memory to know your tennis swing inside and out. Your memory program will interpret these fundamental swing properties as something more to know and to carry with you in your bag.

All swinging actions have a basic nature, which Authentic Tennis refers to as the basic nature of the swing. Authentic Tennis views the swing as a whole, possessing certain reference points or common denominators that illuminate the basic nature of the swing.

These refined references act as guides to help you stay on your path. Authentic Tennis refers to these reference points as the fundamental swing properties. The fundamental swing properties are simply references that show up as the outcome of a natural tennis swing. They are meant to be seen as connected to the swinging process, which cannot be broken down into parts. The mechanical method sees these properties as separate parts that it can use to break down the swing and put it back together again. By breaking the swing down into parts, the parts tend to become more important than the whole. Rather than feeling the oneness of the swing fundamentals, you are thinking about its parts. This leads to treating the parts as the cause of the swing rather than simply the effect of the swing.

The three feel familiar core athletic actions being guided by the aware-feel principles create the foundation of the tennis swing. The basic nature of the tennis swing is made up of the fundamental swing properties. When the aware feel principles move through the three feel familiar core athletic actions, it infuses feel into the technical elements of the tennis swing. These properties are natural references that are easily observable in a natural tennis swing. The swing properties naturally show up. They show up as a further refinement of a natural swinging action. These effects of a natural tennis swing are common to other swinging games and sports. These timeless fundamentals are the result of the basic makeup of the swing. The swing-fundamentals do not change and are inherent to any kind of swinging action. Make no mistake, these fundamentals need to be treated as effects of the swing, not to be over analyzed or seen as the root cause of any swing problem. Swing problems are more related to lack of personal feel than any technical aspect of form. There are many types of swing problems, but there is only one solution. All swing problems are related to lack of awareness in the swinging actions.

A "remember it," "put it together," or mechanical approach views any swing problem as a lack of fundamentals thereby separating cause or personal feel from the fundamentals. Making the fundamental swing properties the cause, treats the body as the cause of the swing rather than the effect. However, the fundamental swing properties can be beneficial in your game, by advancing your understanding of the basic nature of the swing and allowing for further refinement of the swing.

Authentic Tennis presents the fundamental swing properties as an "if list" to add clarity, so that the fundamental swing properties are treated as effects and are what show up as a result of a natural swinging action. There are basic observations, references, or guidelines of any natural swing. The more you are in swing feel the more the fundamental swing properties will show up as natural effects of your personal feel..

The "If" List (Reference Points)

The "If" list, reference points, discussed below are to be focused on, in relationship to the swing being viewed as a whole, a completed action.

1. If you swing naturally, there is a **wrist load, wrist hinge, and wrist release** in the swinging action. In wrist load the racquet is laid back at a 30 to 45 degree angle behind the forearm.

2. With a personal natural swing, there is a target for the swinging action. The **target** exists as a location on the court, as well as a point on the racquet face and as a picture in the mind's eye.

3. In the natural swing, there is a **pendulum** like action, a nearly continuous motion. It allows the preparation, after the shoulder turn, to flow into the forward swing.

4. In the natural swing, there is a **pivot** that joins the body to the swing in the swinging action. The pivot or the turning of the hips takes place as you are contacting the ball.

5. If you swing naturally, there is a **side to front** movement to the swinging action, like a door opening and closing, the swing moves from the side of the body to the front.

6. **Preparation** is a variable and **follow through** is a natural outcome of the swinging action (length = power). Shorter strokes have less potential power and longer strokes have more potential power.

7. In the natural swing, there is a **balance** in the preparation, at contact with the ball, and in the finish of the swinging action. Balance creates a platform for the swing.

8. There is contact with the ball at nearly the **center** of the swinging arc in all natural swings. Note that this could be refined further but is an observable reference point. This point of contact will take place somewhere near the front foot.

9. If you swing naturally there is an **inside-out** swing pattern. The
    racquet head is thrown away from the body utilizing centrifugal
    force commonly referred to as racquet head speed. Your
    swinging action starts inside the ball and just before contact, the
    racquet head is thrown away from the body and continues
    toward the target.

     The mechanical method reverses the cause and effect
relationship of a tennis swing. It treats the body as a machine, making
what shows up in the swing, the fundamental swing properties, as
causal.

     What happens to "feel" when you treat the fundamental
swing properties as causal rather than effect? When you view the
fundamental swing properties as the cause of the swing, feel stops
flowing, becomes fixed and disconnected from the swing form. Once
feel becomes disconnected from the swing form, you end up getting
the look of the swing minus the feel of it. The swing breaks down,
resulting in errors. Feel is the quality that connects the swing to a
natural order, the swing timing as connected to the whole. In
contrast, what happens to "feel" when you treat the fundamental
swing properties as effects? When you treat the fundamental swing
properties as effects of the swing, feel flows throughout the swinging
action, it adapts, and it connects to the swing form. The tennis swing
is experienced as a holistic integrated response, which cannot be
separated or broken down without destroying the feel for the swing.

     The vision of Authentic Tennis is to learn by feel and play by
feel. To learn and play by feel you are going to need to tap into the

art of mindfulness. **Mindfulness** is a deep focus in the present moment with the absence of self-consciousness. Mindfulness strengthens focus and connects the fundamental swing properties to your natural swing. It serves as a bridge in creating an aware or deliberate swing. By being aware of the fundamental swing properties, you will be able to refine your natural swing. Unless you have never played, you have already experienced many of these properties within your tennis strokes. If these core properties are not present within your swing, Authentic Tennis suggests that you become aware of the timeless fundamentals that resonate with you.

Mindfulness vs. Concentration

To gain further insight into using mindfulness for the fundamental swing properties, notice its contrast to the mechanical method of utilizing concentration. Authentic Tennis views the difference between mindfulness and concentration in the same way as the contrasted difference between natural and mechanical. **Concentration** is a forced focus. It programs tension between doing the swinging action right and not doing it wrong. Concentration implies judgment, effort, trying and thinking. Concentration divides experiences, thereby totally manufacturing a resistance to what is. "Concentrate on this, don't concentrate on that", programs a forced focus. This forced focus separates the mind from the body, disconnecting the body from its continuous feel flow. Concentration is over hyped in the mechanical method and is a tool used to habitually program the swing. We suggest that it is not the final answer.

Authentic Tennis defines mindfulness as paying attention without interfering or trying. **Mindfulness** is a one pointed attention, yet it is passive and receptive by nature. Mindfulness does not separate the focus of attention from the overall feel of the swinging action. You can be mindful of a fundamental swing property without making it primary. Mindfulness has a receptive quality that allows without trying. Mindfulness serves to expand feel rather than to inhibit it.

When the fundamental swing properties are missing in your swing, Authentic Tennis uses the passive approach of mindfulness to focus on the missing fundamental swing property. This passive approach does not separate the mind from the body, unlike thinking which does separate the mind from body. It also does not separate the aware-feel principles from the form of the swing. Take for example, the fundamental swing property of wrist load, wrist hinge, and wrist release. When you are mindful of wrist load or laying the wrist back, the wrist hinge and wrist release will occur naturally off of the feel familiar side arm throwing motion. Wrist load will produce solid hand contact and the racquet head will sweep through the ball. This demonstrates the most essential relationship in an Authentic swing. Note that wrist load, wrist hinge and wrist release applies to all strokes accept the volley, which does not release the wrist through the ball after contact. So, if you are missing the feel of wrist load, wrist hinge, and wrist release and your swing does not feel solid, you can become mindful of this property and still stay connected to a relaxed swinging action, not separating form from feel. The relaxed focus of mindfulness allows for integrating any swing property into the total swing feel.

Apply the mental state of unattached mindfulness and connect it to the three feel familiar athletic actions. Mindfulness can be used to integrate any of the fundamental swing properties that resonate with you. As you become more mindful of the feel familiar core athletic actions and their connection to the fundamental swing properties, you will sense the aware-feel principles flowing throughout the swing. Your auditory, visual, and kin-esthetic senses will be enhanced. A sense of no unnecessary tension, as if the ball is just in the way of the swing, will be experienced. You will feel a racquet head and hand connection that allows you to sense the hand racquet head position throughout the swing. There will be a natural feeling of the amount of energy and swing length based on the target. The line of energy toward the target will be sensed by the mind's eye. The Seeing Eye will observe the ball more clearly. There will be a feeling of natural rhythm and timing to the side arm throwing motion, upward throwing motion, and catching motion. There will be a sense of contact at the center of the swing arc. There will be a sense of spatial awareness so the ball does not invade the space of a free relaxed swinging motion. There will be a sense of **absorbing** the ball on the racquet strings and **propelling** it forward. There will be a time and distance awareness, which allows you to vary swing length based on position and time. When the swinging action is in "feel", the fundamental swing properties occur naturally. They tap into the creative process- the state that is associated with peak performance. This is the miracle of effortless skill taking place. Get ready to discover the power of your natural state!

5 NATURAL LEARNING:
THE POWER OF PEAK PERFORMANCE

SO FAR ON YOUR journey to your Authentic swing you have experienced tennis as a game of the hand. You have experienced the three feel familiar core athletic actions that create a natural rhythm and timing for the five basic tennis strokes. You have noticed how the aware feel principles have guided you toward greater swing feel. You have further refined your strokes by becoming mindful of the fundamental swing properties.

If you have been on the mechanical method, you have copied the perfect swing model and you have memorized the countless details that makeup the strokes. People say that you have excellent form but you wonder why you are so inconsistent.

Hopefully, you have had enough trust and faith to stay on the path of Authentic Tennis and not be tempted by the mechanical method. If so, it is time to reap the rewards, accelerate your learning, and experience the power of peak performance.

If you happen to have remained on the path of the mechanical method, in order to accelerate your learning, you are going to need to find new methods, a new book, or a new teacher to keep up with the constantly updated "modern game" program.

To this point in your journey to your Authentic swing, you have been using the power of mindfulness to connect with the feel of your strokes. This has likely lead to a greater sense of feel familiarity with them. The benefits of mindfulness cannot be over expressed. It is essential to use mindfulness in order to transition into a peak performance state. As you maintain a consistent mindfulness of your tennis swing you may cross over into an effortless, balanced, intuitive, adaptive, and flexible state. You have just entered the **peak performance state**, sometimes referred to as **the zone**. No amount of trying or concentration will produce the peak performance state. Peak performance shows up when there is deep focus in the present moment on what you are doing, like swinging your tennis racquet. Miraculously, you cross a mental threshold and the gift of peak performance, your natural feel state, appears.

The peak performance state lies outside the thinking mind, the instrument of the known. It is an observer mode of higher consciousness, which cannot be reproduced or replicated. Since peak performance lies outside the thinking mind it cannot be captured, possessed or conditioned by thought. In the peak performance state, the unconditioned mind is united with the body, creating a sense of oneness between the experience and the one who experiences. It is a holistic state where mind, body and spirit are integrated in the present moment. The subject and object of any experience becomes unified rather than separated. When you are in the zone or peak performance state, improvement can take a quantum leap. Peak performance is a receptive state, often referred to in Eastern Philosophy as "no mind" or consciousness minus thought. This state integrates the unknown feel with the known form. Any attempt to control this peak performance state takes you out of it. Once thinking enters the picture, peak performance disappears. Thinking initiates trying and trying neutralizes awareness—the peak performance state.

If peak performance is the most powerful learning state for all physical action like the tennis swing, why are we not tapping into it, to accelerate the learning process? The answer to this question lies in recognizing the difference between the ego, (past or future mind), and our natural state, the power of the present.

The **ego**, simply put, is who you think you are. The ego perceives itself as separate from everyone and everything, even experience itself. The ego distances itself from the present by identifying itself with the past and thinking about the future. It looks to the past for its identity and to the future for its gratification. The present represents a kind of death to the ego because it loses its identity within it. Unfortunately for the ego, accelerated learning through the natural peak performance state only takes place in the present. However, this does not stop the ego from trying to capture it, possess it, claim ownership for it, and control it.

The ego programs the past into mental emotional reactive patterns that becomes habitual ways of thinking, feeling, and acting. Almost like an animal, (Pavlov's dogs), our mental and emotional reactions become inflexible, predictable, and automatic. We normally do not pay a lot of attention to our programming because we associate our programming with who we think we are. To maintain, develop, and actualize our ego identity, we stay locked up in our mental emotional reactive patterns, becoming a prisoner to our habits. Habit and deliberate aware action cannot co-exist. The ego and its conditioned force of habit become so strong that it programs a kind of inertia, blocking our ability to change. We often end up using the same ineffective habitual action over and over again and expecting a different result. This is often described as the definition of insanity. The ego's past programming just keeps on manufacturing future experience, until our life and tennis strokes feel like the movie *Ground Hog Day*—same old, same old, over and over.

The peak performance state allows you to bypass your programmed habits, accelerate your learning and transform your tennis swing. You do not have to be a highly trained athlete to access this relaxed, alert present mental state. Likewise, you do not have to be a highly trained athlete to experience the accelerated learning benefits of this peak performance state. The miracle of the present is that it unifies experience creating no duality between observation and the observer or the subject and the object of any experience. You could describe it as the feeling of oneness with your swing.

The conventional method of programming the tennis swing through memory does not lead to peak performance. The conventional method that applies learning through information and memory is often referred to as directed learning. You are familiar with directed learning as it is the primary tool used for teaching in the school system. It involves memorization of information then later being tested on what you can remember. This type of learning has value in many areas of life, particularly in informational settings where recalling information is primary. However, this type of learning is not nearly as valuable in teaching a physical skill, like swinging a racquet. Feeling the swing is much more valuable than knowing how the swing works.

The mechanical method of teaching tennis treats the swing the same way as learning information in schools. It uses memorization of steps starting from something you know, like 1+1=2, and then builds off of that, 2+1=3, 3+1=4, and so forth. When applying the mechanical method to teach tennis you might be asked to remember that getting ready + preparing + contact + follow through + finish = the swing you want. The belief is by knowing the swing and memorizing it you can reproduce it. There is no feel to this method because the thinking mind becomes split from what the body is experiencing. Peak performance is the experience of unifying the mind and body, your accelerated learning state.

The directed learning method appeals to the ego because the ego thinks by knowing more it will become more. The more you apply knowing to the tennis swing the less likely you are to feel and be aware of what you are doing. Thinking about the tennis swing just keeps adding more steps, confusion, and complication. The cluttered thinking mind is the problem. Knowing more can become a roadblock to physical learning, as thinking and feeling are mutually exclusive. Thinking separates the doer from the thinker, neutralizing the observer mode of consciousness-the peak performance state. The observer state of consciousness allows for continuous non-judgmental feedback and is self-correcting.

If you have played tennis before, is it any wonder that the strokes that you have the most trouble with are the ones that you have probably put the most thought into? The stroke/strokes that are easiest for you have probably been the ones that you have put the least amount of thought into, making them the most natural. So you could ask yourself this question if you are having difficulty with a tennis stroke; Am I thinking about the stroke because I am struggling with it or am I struggling with the stroke because I am thinking about it? Knowing and thinking, which are the tools of directed learning, do not produce peak performance. For the few players that have been able to convert information into feel and reach the world class level, there have been thousands of players that have come nowhere near reaching their potential. Authentic Tennis poses the question, has anyone ever reached their potential? We suggest that regardless of ability level, as your feel expands so will your potential.

Learning, in general, is a natural response to the need to grow. Nature possesses a natural evolutionary intention to evolve. Intention shapes action in the physical world. You can tap into this natural evolutionary process through the vehicle of playful discovery. However, before tapping into the vehicle of playful discovery, you need the intention to learn and improve naturally. The natural approach to learning uses the art of playful discovery. Authentic Tennis refers to this natural approach as playful discovery because you are literally playing around with the swing and having fun while doing it. Playful discovery is an inside out process which allows you to learn for yourself rather than someone telling you how to do it or what to do. Authentic Tennis is not suggesting that a tennis coach could not be a valuable asset in guiding your attention and awareness to shaping your swing and game. However, no one but you can be in touch with your personal feel. All learning is self-learning and when you learn something for yourself you are more highly motivated. The playful discovery process is mindfulness in action with mindfulness naturally transitioning into the peak performance state.

The art of playful discovery process uses the natural learning processes of trial and error, feedback and overcompensation, using both ends of an action to find the middle. Trial and error works off of an action awareness feedback loop. This process is evident when you watch a young child first learning to ride a bike. As the child begins to roll forward he may lean too far to the left and fall over. The next time he gets on his bike and rolls forward he may feel his body leaning to the left, then overcompensate to the right falling over in that direction. The child is sensing feedback on the nature of balance and using the natural learning process of overcompensation, using both ends of a process to find the middle. As the child begins to ride his bike and move between these two extremes, he will find the middle or center point and obtain a sense of balance. This is the natural process of acquiring feel familiarity-when I do this, this happens and when I do that, that happens. Eventually the child will be riding effortlessly as he acquires the feel familiarity of balancing his bike. The body will recognize this pattern and natural learning has taken place.

Through the process of trial and error you expand the feel familiarity of your tennis strokes. When you apply trial and error to the tennis swing, it keeps the swing simple by allowing you to feel your way through the process - when my hand does this, this happens and when my hand does that, that happens. You are not demanding the perfect swing, over thinking, or over analyzing how the swing works. The playful discovery process uses trial and error and overcompensation, permitting a more adaptive and flexible approach to the tennis swing. For example, if I am missing too far to the right, let me miss too far to the left. If I am sensing too much tightness in my swing, let me loosen my grip pressure. Playful discovery and trial and error utilize surrendered action, the action of non-resistance. Mistakes are treated as friends and teachers and are only used as feedback in creating your personal best swing.

The rote memory used in directed learning, programs a very mechanical mental state. The mechanical mind conditions a repetitive formula for analyzing experience. It starts by perceiving an object or experience, it identifies it, it makes a note whether it desires or resists the experience, and then it records it. When it comes to peak performance or accelerated learning the mind's past conditioning has no formula for adapting to the ever-changing present moment. In learning a physical skill like the tennis swing, the mechanical mind continually uses repetition to produce what is referred to as muscle memory. A literal interpretation of muscle memory would describe it as a memory coordinated muscle motion. As Authentic Tennis has already emphasized, memory disconnects the form of the tennis swing from the feel of the tennis swing. Memory programmed repetition can condition the form of the swing, but without feel, the tennis swing will not respond effectively to the unique challenges that it is presented with in every swing. If there is a lack of feel with any tennis stroke the mechanical tool of repetition will program that feel deficiency into the stroke. Since there are no two swings exactly the same, repetition and muscle memory, whose goal is to program a uniformed swing, is attempting a task beyond the realm of its program.

Many of you are probably reading this book, Authentic Tennis, to learn the tennis swing, refine the tennis swing, or possibly recreate the tennis swing. Tennis instruction has not helped you; neither have tennis books, magazines, and videos. You may have reached a point of great frustration to the point that you may not believe that swing change is even possible. The mechanical method, using programmed memory and repetition, is the culprit behind your lack of improvement.

Authentic Tennis points you in the direction of peak performance. This holistic state is where your swing can be transformed through the awareness of your actions. It is a state that bypasses your conditioned mental program, overriding repetition and muscle memory, allowing for effortless self-correction. It is time to swing deliberately. The Authentic approach to the tennis swing focuses on what is happening in the present moment. To swing deliberately is to be in the present with all your actions. In reality, the tennis swing always takes place in the present.

When you enter the zone or peak performance state, you feel as though you are observing yourself, like watching a 3D movie at the theater. You sense that peak performance is a gift that you are receiving and you are simply a vehicle for its expression. This state is the most powerful way to accelerate the skills of your ground strokes, your volleys, and your serve. As you become aware of your ability to shift out of your thinking state or memory program, you will enter the peak performance observation state with greater frequency. You have been made aware that peak performance is your natural state and by accessing it, you have the most powerful source available for creating your Authentic swing. Now Authentic Tennis will offer you a framework for expanding your personal feel, which we refer to, as the integrated swing progression.

6 THE INTEGRATED SWING PROGRESSION: THE FRAMEWORK AND EVOLUTION FOR FEEL

YOUR JOURNEY TO FIND your Authentic Tennis swing has been filled with meaningful and interesting experiences. You have been traveling your path with a sense of hand feel, the three familiar core athletic actions, and your friendly feel guides—the aware-feel principles. Your strokes are being refined by using mindfulness to focus on any of the fundamental swing properties you sense are not present or showing up in your swing. You have tapped into the state of peak performance and it is very likely that you are shifting into this state more frequently. How are you feeling? It is now time to take a leap of faith and merge with consciousness itself by allowing your swing to evolve naturally through the integrated swing progression, the natural framework for feel.

If you are still following the mechanical method, you probably are watching your tennis swing on the latest high tech digital 3D TV for swing modeling. You have spent so much time on the details of the swing that you can recite them forwards and backwards. You have searched the Internet for every new method, new teacher, new book, or new video. You have just purchased the latest subscription to biomechanics magazine that emphasizes body mechanics and breaking the swing down with the use of gadgets and the latest exercises for training the body. With all this information and technology at your disposal, you still wonder why you are not improving?

With all the latest scientific advancements and with the mechanical evolution of technology, you might ask yourself this question, is it better to evolve the tennis swing through traditional science or through consciousness, feel, and the natural creative process? The scientific method is defined by Dictionary.Com, as a method of research in which a problem is identified, relevant data gathered, a hypothesis is formulated from the data, and a hypothesis is empirically tested. Science hypothesizes that the universe is created from a beginning point (somewhere in the past) and that it follows a logical sequence of events of causes and effects. If A then B, if B then C and so on. Traditional science holds the belief that whatever caused the universe, happened sometime in the past and can be known, even if it cannot be seen by the naked eye. All traditional scientific theories on the cause of the universe hypothesize from the viewpoint that consciousness is not the cause. They believe that consciousness evolved from the universe rather than the universe evolving from consciousness.

Approaching any problem, like the tennis swing, through the scientific method, will never lead to consciousness. The belief that the scientific method can solve any problem is influencing all areas of life, including tennis instruction. Traditional Science, which has lead to the mechanical method, divorces form from consciousness or feel. Whether or not you believe science can truly solve the mysteries of the universe or human problems, no amount of scientific information will allow you to feel the tennis stroke.

However, when the creative process is perceived as being a byproduct of consciousness (the cause) then the universe becomes an effect. The universe is an expression of the creative process within consciousness. The creative process, consciousness, and feel, all exist in the present and therefore cannot be separated by the past and future. The scientific method can never prove the existence of the present or the now, where consciousness lives. The nature of evidence itself is that it comes from the past. Consciousness creates a feel connectivity that has integrating and unifying qualities to all life and all form, including the tennis swing. The creative process expands the universe through consciousness (feel) the same as the tennis swing expands through consciousness (feel).

The integrated swing progression is an approach for expanding feel by creating a framework for feel through observing the creative process of natural evolution. In the creative process feel or consciousness evolves naturally with a corresponding expansion of form. Form expands as the feel expands. Authentic Tennis uses this natural process to create an Authentic swing that evolves and expands naturally.

To understand the difference between the Authentic
approach of evolving the swing to the mechanical method of reverse
engineering the swing, first, it is essential to understand what reverse
engineering means. Reverse engineering the tennis swing works
backwards, outside-in, or reverse from the creative process. It works
backwards in time making the past causal and disregarding the
present, the natural flow, like a fish that try's and struggles to swim
upstream. Reverse engineering starts at the finished product or
result—the world-class player, for example. By working backwards or
reversed from the finished product of the tennis swing it becomes
necessary to break the swing down into parts in order to teach it.
Reverse engineering the tennis swing puts the cart before the horse.
The cart represents the finished product and the horse represents the
creative process. It attempts to bypass the Authentic creative process
by engineering a replication of the tennis swing. But in reality what
gets bypassed is "feel" itself. The creative process always works
inside-out; you can never duplicate it by reverse engineering it. The
reverse engineering informational method blocks the learning
process. It stops the learning process because it takes you out of the
present moment where the creative process and natural learning takes
place.

Authentic Tennis sees the tennis stroke as an artistic
expression that flows forward from moment to moment. An artist,
like Vincent Van Gogh, created his paintings in a feel state, probably
as if he were observing himself painting. The creative process is a gift

that flows through you. A master artist originates their work the same way a world-class tennis player creates their swing. Can you imagine Vincent Van Gogh painting by the numbers? This is no different than a tennis player learning to stroke the tennis ball though the mechanical method. All great tennis players are feel players.

Consciousness and feel creates intention and shapes form. When you play from consciousness and feel you are working in harmony with the creative process. This allows your tennis swing to be natural and easy like a fish swimming downstream.

Ancient Game vs. Modern Game

What is commonly termed the "modern game" in tennis is a byproduct of the mechanical evolution of the racquet. The powerful racquet has led to an over emphasis of applying force. The modern game advocates learning through the mechanical method, implementing the use of reverse engineering. It builds the tennis swing off a swing model that has been scientifically proven in the past and is continually being updated, based on the latest scientific technology and information. It seeks to duplicate, replicate, or clone the form. The modern game puts form over consciousness (feel), and the past over the present. The modern game leads to the failure to evolve the strokes through the creative process of consciousness and feel.

Extreme body movement and training is used by the modern game, to acquire and apply force to the ball. You can observe such force related effects in the modern game as extreme shoulder rotation, jumping on ground strokes/serves and swinging volleys. This method of load, explode and land is the final thing that you need to learn if you aspire to play at a world-class level. While these techniques can be beneficial to reach the highest level, these complex body actions are the last 10-15% of refining the swing. The modern game's method takes on a more one-dimensional focus rather than developing a feel foundation for a relaxed swing. It is pulled toward the concepts of "get stronger, hit harder, and swing faster." The modern game treats what are the extreme effects of the body as more important than personal feel. Like the movie "Star Wars", this is turning tennis into the clone wars. The more the modern game moves away from consciousness and feel the more tennis clones are manufactured.

The Authentic Tennis approach aligns to the creative process, the source of all form. Just as tennis began as the game of the hand with its focus on feel, it still remains so today. Authentic Tennis realizes this in an aware mental state, the body's wisdom instinctively feels its way towards the Authentic swing. This creates a unique personal feel and individual variations form. Authentic strokes are byproducts of natural swinging actions which make every stroke a unique work of art. Authentic Tennis puts feel before form and treats the present as the only point where feel and consciousness exist and creativity can take place. It views the game as multidimensional where expression is unlimited and new players add their own personal flavor and unique expression to the tennis swing. Authentic Tennis moves from consciousness and feel, the artist within you, to your Authentic swing masterpiece.

The Evolutionary Framework for Feel

Before Authentic Tennis reveals the integrated swing progression, which will expand your personal feel and align your swing with the natural creative process, it is essential to understand the way nature evolves. Nature evolves through consciousness and natural order, just like a baby learns to crawl, walk and run. Everything in nature is integrated and connected to the whole. Natural evolution is a continuous process where any result is simply part of the process. Natural evolution moves, expands, and evolves continuously; there is no fixed or permanent form or stops and starts, because it is always evolving. Authentic Tennis realizes this by moving forward or flowing with the creative process. There is no need to break the swing down into parts. Each swing that is taken helps to evolve the tennis stroke as long as you are in feel or your natural state. When it comes to evolving the tennis swing there is no way to feel. Feel is the way. Anytime that you disconnect from feel you have moved away from natural evolution.

To create a framework for feel, it is essential to recognize the natural order of evolution and the relationships of simple to complex, small before big and short before long. Nature moves from simple to complex. Simple allows for progression and evolution. Simple naturally moves towards complex, this is the basic nature of the evolutionary process. The more elements that need to be integrated into the creative process the more complex the evolution.

In nature, you do not see a butterfly turning into a caterpillar or a frog turning into a tadpole. When you start from simple, the complex takes care of itself. As a natural consequence of moving from simple to complex, the relationships of short before long and small before big are inherent to the creative process. These relationships are all natural principles that originate from observing the creative process. To evolve the tennis swing, Authentic Tennis starts with the volley as it is the simplest motion with the least amount of movement to integrate. It is the shortest motion with the racquet head being closer to the ball. It trains the smaller muscles, the hand and the wrist before invoking the bigger muscles of the body. Deliberate hand action takes precedence over the body in feeling the Authentic swing.

The relationship between the racquet head and the ball is the most primary relationship in an Authentic swing. It is the racquet head's feel relationship to the hand as applied to the ball, which sends the ball to the target. The racquet head swings behind the ball and moves through the ball for all swinging actions. When the racquet head is applied to the ball there is solid contact as a consequence of flat hand feel and timing. This principle is easier to apply on shorter strokes where the racquet head is nearer to the oncoming ball. The farther away the racquet head is from the ball, the more complex the action. The shorter volley strokes create a platform for success, allowing for the feeling of solid contact as the racquet head moves behind and through the ball. There is a oneness of fundamentals that serve as common denominators in all swinging actions. The short stroke of the volley (the catching motion), serves as a foundation for the longer strokes; the ground strokes (the side arm throwing motions) and the serve (upward throwing motion). The volley, the simplest motion, is the easiest to learn because it involves less racquet and body motion. The volley is like a baby crawling, the ground strokes like a young child walking, and the serve is like the child running. This is the natural evolutionary process. It is how feel and consciousness expand.

The Integrated Swing Progression

The integrated swing progression can either be practiced alone by tossing the ball up or dropping it, or with a friend tossing or stroking balls to you. While the integrated swing progression is very simple, it will have a profound effect for players of every level.   It is the natural progression to expanding personal feel for the swing.

1. Authentic Tennis recommends that you integrate swing feel by starting with the volley- the shortest whole stroke. Begin fairly close to the net with the eastern grip. Keep the target for your volleys inside the service line to start with. You will gain a feel for the racquet head, like a hammer to a nail, behind the ball, and slightly through the ball. This is a very short stroke similar to the game of patty cake that you played as a child.

2. As you gain a feel for the volley (the catching motion), move back to the service line. Use your forehand and backhand ground strokes to expand (lengthen) your swing slightly and stroke the ball from your service line to the opposing service line on the

other side of the net. There will be slightly more propelling feeling with this stroke. It is rumored that many of the former top Australian players played a game inside the service lines called dink. This game improves feel for the racquet head's application to the ball and is also a great form of exercise and a lot of fun. It allows players of every level to practice together, much like a handicap in golf. There is only one rule for dink and that is you must stroke the ball gently. Any ball played with too much speed is considered to be unfair "dinkum." Enjoy dink as it builds feel, sensitivity, consistency and touch for your ground strokes.

3. As you become more consistent for stroking the ball over short distances, move back to three quarters court. This is half the distance between the service line and the baseline. The farther you move back in the court, the more you gradually lengthen your ground strokes. Gradually lengthen your ground strokes in order to propel the ball over the net and behind the opposing service line but in front of the three quarters target or player that you are rallying with. Be mindful of matching the energy to the task.

4. Stay aware that you are stroking the ball not hitting it. Solid contact and a relaxed swing are the cornerstones of the Authentic swing.

5. Finally, move back to the baseline. Use a long natural swing, as if you are throwing the ball side arm from one baseline to the opposing baseline, to propel the ball over the net. The length and

looseness of the swing creates distance, not swinging hard at the ball. Treat the ball like a valued pet, stroke it; don't hit it. Keep the racquet and hand as primary and the body as secondary. Feel the buildup of momentum as the racquet head effortlessly sweeps through the ball and releases toward the target.

6. It is now time to experience the stroke that starts the point and is the most complex and the longest of the tennis strokes, the serve or upward throwing motion. Start sideways to the net in a throwing position with the racquet head behind your ear. It is beneficial to begin by starting at the service line to shorten distance and remove excessive effort. Start off gently serving the ball diagonally into the opposing service box. As you begin to consistently feel a relaxed upward throwing motion, take one step back at a time and gradually work your way back to the baseline. Don't be in a hurry. Rome was not built in a day and neither was the serve. As your motion becomes relaxed and you are consistently serving into the service boxes, it is time to experiment with a longer service motion by combining the toss and the swing. Start sideways to the net with the racquet hand and tossing hand at chest level in front of your body. There are many ways the service preparation can be done. The simplest approach is where the two hands go down together and swing up together in a pendulum like motion. Your personal feel will suggest a longer or shorter preparation to get the racquet head comfortably behind your ear in a natural throwing position.

Throw the racquet head up and out through the ball and let the natural wrist release send the ball into the service box.

The integrated swing progression simply aligns to the creative process. It is meant to be a reference for naturally evolving your swing. Do not let it become a rigid program or rule that restricts you from exploring your personal feel. Enjoy the process of naturally expanding your feel. Value each stroke you take without over analyzing it or focusing on the results. Over attachment to results will produce swing tension. Just feel it! The integrated swing progression will serve as a framework to create, expand and reconnect to personal feel.

The next chapter, Authentic Practice, Awareness in Action, will get you ready to take your game to a whole new level.

7 AUTHENTIC PRACTICE: AWARENESS IN ACTION

YOUR JOURNEY TO CREATE your Authentic swing has taken you through a self-discovery process. You have discovered the feel relationship between the hand and the racquet head. You have become intimate with the three feel familiar athletic actions, which serve as a foundation for a natural swing. You have become more aware of your personal feel by applying the aware-feel principles to your tennis strokes. You have further refined your swing with the fundamental swing properties. You have accelerated your ability to learn and feel the swing through the power of peak performance. You are applying the integrated swing progression to expand feel, naturally aligning to the creative process. Now it is time to totally let go of any past programming and step into the illuminating light of aware-doing. To merge with the force of nature, your path will need to take a remarkable galactic twist. You are, in a way, entering another dimension of time and space, you are entering the present.

The present is where you are connected to the creative force of nature. Just as in the movie Star Wars, Luke Sky Walker used the "force" to balance and unify the universe. So too, does Authentic Tennis use the force of nature to unify and balance your Authentic swing. "Let the force be with you" (the force of nature). It is time to embark on your Jedi training.

If you are still struggling along the mechanical path, let's review what has happened to you. You started your journey by trying to replicate the perfect swing model. You spent hours programming your swing.

You have chosen science and its analytical method. You have bought into the modern game and how different it appears than the way tennis used to be played. You are looking for more gadgets and bio-mechanical methods to train your body. You may have given up hope that any change is possible in your tennis strokes. So, if you have continued along the mechanical path, you have embarked on a journey that has lead you toward the dark side (the force of habit). It has led you to the supreme programming of mechanical evolution, where groups of robots, known as clones, are fighting the forces of good.

The mechanical method has a primary influence on all areas of life, including learning the tennis swing and how to play the game. The mechanical method, with its emphasis on repetition and programming, is the widely accepted belief on how everything is taught and practiced. Just because something has been taught a certain way for a long period of time, does not mean that there is not a better way. Many players have lost interest and are burned out on this "try harder," "more is better" belief. The mechanical method assumes that if you memorize all the swing steps and work hard enough at the tennis swing that you will automatically master it. It believes that repetition is the master skill. It treats practice as simply a means to an end-winning. Practice turns into drudgery; something a player must do in order to get good. Struggle, sweat, and tears are the price for greatness. Do the tennis swing over and over again in a uniform way until it becomes automatic, is the battle cry. However, human nature has the desire to experience new things, which turns forced swing repetition into a grind, something a player does not look forward to—a keep working or you won't get better- attitude. The boring nature of forced repetition imposes an albatross (burden) around the player's neck. Much like a dog being conditioned to run to his bowl when the owner shakes the dog food bag, the mechanical method wants you to turn on your "computer stroking program" as you see the ball coming. See the ball, run to the ball, hit the ball, and repeat. The mechanical method expects your strokes to function efficiently even when your personal feel is being blocked.

Authentic practice is deeply rooted in the present moment, turning the tennis swing into an art form, an experience of your own personal feel. Authentic Tennis makes the practice of the swing a process of aware doing. Aware doing is the master skill. Authentic practice brings to the tennis court the three feel familiar athletic actions, the aware-feel principles, the fundamental swing properties, the power of peak performance, and the integrated swing progression. Use these in your practice sessions. In Authentic practice the quality of practice is much more important than the quantity. A half an hour of aware doing practice is better than three hours of forced repetition practice. Quality practice only takes place when you are mindful or present with your actions. Authentic Tennis treats practice as a playful experience, an end in itself. Enjoy the process and the results will take care of themselves. The fun and enjoyment, experienced with continuous personal growth, inspires a love for the game and swing, which serves as a constant motivation for improvement. There are no ordinary swings in Authentic practice; each swing is a unique expression of who you are. Authentic practice creates a direct experience, as it bypasses the conditioned mechanical program. It's simple intention is to be aware of your physical actions. Being aware of the hand, the swing, and the body and allowing the creative process to be natural, effortless, and simple will continually integrate feel into your personal swing. Authentic players look forward to every moment they can spend creating their natural swing. There is never a sense of boredom, repetition, drudgery, grind it out, and keep on working on it. Authentic practice is all about the process (what you can feel), not the results (what happens). When practicing Authentically, use the simple feel test; when you **feel** it you are doing it. Feeling is the foundation for mastery.

Before beginning Authentic practice, Authentic Tennis suggests that you start with a mindfulness check.

Mindfulness Check

1. Begin by noticing what your body is feeling. Notice what parts of your body are holding tension. Becoming aware of tension in the body will naturally dissolve it.

2. Secondly, become mindful of your thoughts. Observe your thinking. Recognize that you are not your thinking program. This will allow you to shift into your natural feeling state. Very often, the tension the mind imposes on the body goes unnoticed.

3. Finally, become aware of how you're feeling inside. Do you sense your emotions flowing freely or do you feel emotions like frustration, anxiety, and anger restricting your feel? As you observe your emotional state, any restrictions blocking the flow of energy will dissolve.

Mindfulness raises your consciousness, so your body, mind, and emotions will work in harmony in a free relaxed state.

Authentic practice, which we define as awareness in action, offers a series of exercises for you to do, notice, and feel. These do, notice, and feel exercises will raise your consciousness, likely advancing your skill level to new heights of personal feel and excellence.

Do, Notice, and Feel Exercises

As you are stroking the tennis ball:

1. Notice and feel your racquet head throughout the swing, particularly just before contact and at contact. Feel the relaxed sweeping action through the ball.

2. Notice and feel any unnecessary tension in your swing. Is your swing relaxed, smooth, and flowing?

3. Pick several different targets on the court and notice your degree of accuracy. Feel if your body and swing allow you to match the energy to the task.

4. Notice if you are sensing a line of energy in the mind's eye, allowing your seeing eyes to focus on the point of contact with the ball.

5. Notice the three feel familiar athletic actions creating a natural rhythm and timing for your stroke.

6. As you are stroking the tennis ball, notice if you feel too close or too far away from the ball. Notice if the contact is a comfortable distance from the body without feeling cramped or over reaching.

7. As you prepare to stroke the tennis ball, do you notice the ball leaving the other player's racquet? Sense the amount of time available to make your swing. Does it necessitate a longer or shorter motion?

8. Notice that on the shorter swings if there is more of a sense of absorbing and redirecting the opponents shot and on the longer swings you are propelling the ball more, using more of your own energy.

9. Notice when the ball bounces if you are watching the ball spinning. This will increase your visual awareness.

10. Notice the sound of the ball on the strings, feeling when the contact with the ball is on or off center of the racquet head.

11. Notice the feel of the ball on the strings; use your hands and fingers to enhance the feel of the stroking action.

12. Notice the feel of the hand moving forward, followed by the racquet head contacting the ball.

13. Notice if the swing length connects to a target on the other side of the net.

14. Notice if the swinging action is moving continuously, creating a rhythm where the preparation flows into the forward swing.

15. Notice if there is a natural pivoting motion on contact, allowing your body to respond to the target.

16. Notice if your preparation or back swing varies and your follow through is a natural outcome.

17. Notice if your body moves side to front like opening and closing a door.

18. Notice your balance throughout the swing. Notice your balance at preparation, at contact and at the finish of the swing.

19. Notice if you are mindful at the point of contact with the ball, often called the moment of truth. It is the moment that many players are not present and tend to look where they are stroking the ball too early.

20. Notice if your swing is moving away from your body, naturally creating racquet head speed.

21. Notice if your swing is creating a natural lifting action, so the ball crosses the net.

22. Notice if the contact with the ball is nearly at the center of the swinging arc.

23. Notice the grip pressure that you have on the handle of your racquet. Often grip pressure is too tight not allowing for a natural wrist and hand motion.

24. Notice your breath. Breathe in on the preparation and breathe out as you start the forward swing; breathing short circuits tension.

25. Notice the tempo or the rate which you accelerate your swing; if it is quick or gradual.

26. Notice if you feel rigidness or tension in the swing.

27. Notice if you feel a wrist load, a wrist hinge, and a wrist release in the swinging action.

28. As you stroke the tennis ball notice if your swing finish feels relaxed.

Deliberate Error Exercises

Deliberate error exercises are exercises that allow you to maintain your feel focus while freeing you from habit.

1. If your stroke is going too short, deliberately stroke the next shot too long.

2. If your shot is going too far to the right of the target, deliberately stroke the ball too far to the left.

3. If your shot has too much force, deliberately use too little force.

By constantly moving between too much and too little you are not reinforcing errors.

Continually making the same mistakes turns errors into habits. A deliberate error is not a habit and therefore does not produce frustration. By moving back and forth between two extremes you will catch the feel of your stroke intention.

Deliberate Stroking Exercises

Deliberate stroking exercises are designed to create a greater awareness for swing feel. Deliberate stroking involves performing the swing in slow motion. The human tendency is to rush through physical actions including the tennis strokes. Rushing will produce errors. The tendency to rush can be eliminated by practicing the swings at slower speed. Awareness will correct errors. Slow the practice swing down like a Tai Chi movement. The slower swinging actions create greater awareness and feel familiarity of the motion. Later, when the swing motions are performed at a quicker tempo, the slow motion feel will carry over into the faster stroke. Practice your swing in slow motion while focusing on taking a relaxed swinging action. Be aware of your hand and racquet head motion throughout the swing. Practice deliberate stroking using your volley, ground strokes, and serving motions. Create your own feel based exercises.

Another deliberate exercise is to use a mirror to view your tennis strokes. See if what you think is happening in your swing is actually what is happening. It is often quoted that a picture is worth a thousand words. Seeing your swing bypasses your conditioned program that may have manufactured ineffective habits that you are not aware of. Again, focus on taking a relaxed swing. Be aware of the hand and racquet head motion.

Self Help Stroke Change: How to Change a Stroke

The mechanical method looks to the outside for someone to fix the stroke, without the players themselves being aware of the cause of the problem. Very often this method leads to a reverse effect. When you try to change something in your swing, without a feel familiarity for fundamentals the stroke you want to change actually gets worse. This has lead to many players losing enjoyment of the game and possibly quitting. Authentic Tennis suggests a simple approach to stroke change.

1. Be aware of and acknowledge a committed intention to change.
2. Be with what is. Stroke the ball without any mental comments about what is right or wrong with your swing.
3. Be mindful of aware-feel principle or a fundamental swing property you wish to integrate.
4. Use self inquiry. Did the action match the intention? Optional, keep an awareness chart of the number of times that you are not mindful of the fundamental swing properties. Be mindful of not being mindful.
5. Stroke with an empty mind for around 10 minutes and allow your natural awareness to catch up with the skill. If awareness and feel are not at the level of the skill or principle you are practicing, change and improvement will not happen.

Stroke Change – Applying the Aware Feel Principles

1. Intention - The desire to stroke the ball more relaxed

2. Aware-feel principle - no unnecessary tension particularly in the shoulder, arm, and hand.

3. Stroke some tennis balls without changing anything - get in touch with your swing.

4. Keep stroking the ball being mindful of your grip pressure and having a relaxed finish to your swing.

5. Self inquiry - Did your stroking action feel more relaxed? Assess your swing on a scale from 1-5, 5 being most tense and 1 being most relaxed.

6. As your swing begins to feel more comfortable let your awareness naturally connect your intention or aware-feel principle to the stroke. Count the number of times you are not mindful of your stroking intention. Awareness corrects error.

Stroke Change – Applying the Fundamental Swing Properties

1. Intention - To make a more balanced stroke. Fundamental swing property – To be balanced throughout the stroke.

2. Stroke some balls without changing anything; get in touch with your balance.

3. Keep stroking and be mindful of your balance throughout the swing.

4. Self inquiry - Did you feel off balance anywhere in the swing? Freeze at the end of your swing and notice your balance. Stroke some balls, if possible, bare footed to feel more grounded and

balanced. Count the number of times you feel off balance and make a note.

5. Practice for about 10 minutes with an empty mind. Let your awareness catch up and integrate with the fundamental swing property you are working on. Awareness will connect balance to your Authentic swing.

This process can be used for any habit in life that you wish to change.

Now you are ready for the acid test, using your relaxed Authentic swing in the arena of competition. Chapter Nine suggests a higher conscious vision for competition allowing your opponent to be an ally instead of an enemy.

8 PLAYING THE GAME OF TENNIS: THE AUTHENTIC VISION OF COMPETITION

NOW THAT YOU HAVE aligned your practice to the force of nature (Jedi training) you are ready for a new mission. Go out on the tennis court and demonstrate the skills of a Jedi tennis master. Your skills include mindfulness, the aware-feel principles, fundamental swing properties, observer mode or peak performance, expanded feel and the ability to evolve the tennis strokes. Bring all these qualities with you into playing the game of tennis.

If you have been on the mechanical method you have been fully programmed and are now a certified clone warrior. Your clone warrior tools include an exact replication of some other players swing. You have become disconnected from your personal feel. You are fully identified with your muscle memory program. You are a robotic creature of habit. You have brought all your technology to the tennis court.

But if you have discovered your Authentic swing, it is time to apply your swing to competition on the court. To play the game of tennis, it is obvious that you are going to need to move to the ball. Authentic Tennis deliberately did not mention footwork in this book. A natural tennis swing is the primary focus, especially in the beginning, learning stages of tennis. Authentic Tennis suggests that the swing is the foundation for footwork, not the footwork is the foundation for the swing. We are not discounting the importance of footwork to the game; however, it is the racquet head that delivers its message to the ball. It is the mission of Authentic Tennis to empower you to create your personal Authentic swing. Footwork, for the most part is very natural, just like walking and running. Footwork appears to work independently of the swing but in reality it is part of the swinging process as connected to the ball. In tennis, the ball is a note and it influences both the length of preparation and the footwork. Like a drummer moving the foot pedals of the drum independently from the drumsticks; both the drum pedals and the drum sticks coordinate to the music and are interdependent on each other. Likewise, the hands and feet create a rhythm for your Authentic swing based on ball speed.

Before you go on the tennis court, Authentic Tennis suggests a vision for competition, which will allow you to play your best tennis. This new vision for competition is already present in many people's consciousness. It is the realization that working together creates a scenario where the whole becomes greater than the sum of its parts. The parts help the whole and the whole helps the parts. It is much like workers who invest in the company they work for. When there is a sense of sharing in the overall success of the company, there is a tendency for people to work up to their potential. As people expand their own productivity, the company as a whole, becomes more successful and in return the individual benefits from the whole. In the same way, when you view you and your opponent on the tennis court as a whole and not separate, it contributes to the success of both players. When competition is used to bring out the best in each other, the tennis match is immediately transformed into an experience of fun, appreciation, and an environment that moves beyond past limitations. The challenge of each player to do their best, allows the other player to reach beyond their personal standards. The tennis game then becomes a win-win situation for both players, regardless of outcome. Both players sense that they have given their best.

Using the mechanical method, competition becomes a matter of personal survival. You have heard this term coined to describe the NCAA single elimination basketball tournament; survive and advance. The survival mentality views competition or teams as antagonists, where they are pitted against each other in a kind of battle or war. My force must be better than your force. Rather than seeing competition as a challenge, it is viewed as a threat, almost like a life or death situation. Vince Lombardi was famously quoted as saying, "winning isn't everything, it is the only thing". This result oriented approach leads to trying, tension, and over control and makes competition more a relief of not losing, rather than the simple joy of competition. This view manufactures a duality where the losers look bad and the winners look good. "To the winners goes the spoils" and "nobody remembers who came in second" are common beliefs in the antagonistic view of competition.

Authentic Tennis recognizes the inherent challenges in a competitive situation. These challenges and distractions include but are not limited to the list below. How you respond to these challenges and distractions depends on whether you approach them as an **ego tennis player** or an **Authentic Tennis player.**

Below are some examples of how the ego tennis player and the Authentic Tennis player deal with the same circumstances.

1. **Opponents you don't get along with.** The **ego tennis player** sees opponents it does not get along with as a threat to its survival. This antagonistic viewpoint of the ego wants to dominate and destroy their opponent and is afraid their opponent will dominate and destroy them. This "go against" attitude manufactures a tension between mind and body. This tension is reflected on the court through errors, lack of feel, poor decision making, and break downs of the technical and tactical awareness which is needed to play the game. For the **Authentic Tennis player,** the opponent is viewed as a challenge, an enjoyable contest where the ability to stay relaxed and focused is the top priority. The Authentic Tennis player demonstrates their stroking skill set, focusing on the process of a relaxed swing, without being overly concerned about their opponent. Freeing attention from viewing the opponent as a threat allows the

Authentic player to perform in a feel state, which unifies technical and tactical awareness consistently reducing errors.

2. **A partner in doubles who constantly criticizes you.** Many of you who have played tennis for awhile have probably played doubles matches with a fault-finding partner. probably played doubles matches with a fault-finding partner. The ego tennis player's tendency is to place blame when things are not going well. Rather than viewing the partnership as a whole, the ego player wishes to separate himself/herself and not be responsible for the losing effort. The ego player thinks by being negative he/she can solve problems. The end result is usually a situation that amounts to three against one, the two opponents and your partner against you. When you approach this scenario as an ego player you will either react by trying too hard and doing too much or viewing the situation as hopeless, thereby giving up. The Authentic Tennis player recognizes that doubles is a team sport and that you cannot be successful without both players working together in an environment of acceptance. This famous quote is a good example—"there is no "I" in team." To turn around this potential spiral, it is essential for the Authentic player to communicate with the nit-picking player in a heartfelt way. If the criticizing partner does not respond to this honest interaction then you may need to choose a different partner in the future. If your partner remains critical, do your best. Avoid taking things personally and let the criticism roll of your body, like water rolling off a duck's back.

3. **Excessive heat, cold, and wind**. When you play tennis you
    may encounter excessive heat, cold, or wind. These might
    become the conditions of contest on any given day. The ego
    tennis player may have indoctrinated a conditioned program that
    views these environmental conditions as a threat to the ability to
    perform. The ego player may start the match, without giving
    these conditions much thought. When the ego player starts
    losing, he/she may blame the weather, (the conditions of
    contest) for the poor performance. The Authentic Tennis player
    embraces the environmental conditions of contest. They
    recognize by being with what is, it will allow them to play their
    best tennis. They view these excessive environmental elements as
    a creative challenge and something to be used in a way that will
    facilitate their play. The Authentic player recognizes that it is the
    same environmental conditions for both players. It is essential to
    be flexible and as it is commonly quoted "when God gives you
    lemons make lemonade."

4. **The desire to win and not to lose**. The ego tennis player views
    tennis as a win or lose situation. Either I am better than you or I
    am worse. This duality leads to over control using excessive
    effort either to win or not to lose. Unfortunately this rarely
    works out because excessive effort and "trying" imposes tension
    on the body causing a player not to play up to their potential.
    The Authentic Tennis player does not view the game from a
    dualistic viewpoint. They view winning and losing as inherent to
    the sport. To the Authentic Tennis player doing their best, taking

care of each stroke, making a relaxed swing, and being mindful of the point of contact are the key to their performance. The Authentic player always feels good regardless of the outcome; with a personal understanding that they played the best they could on that day.

5. **The score.** The ego tennis player is preoccupied with the score. This preoccupation with the score is another way the ego player avoids the present, keeping itself in a thinking state, disconnected from the swing. The score usually influences the ego players emotional state, feeling inflated when they are winning and deflated when they are losing. Pumping the fist or throwing the racquet are expressions of these two extremes. The ego wants to feel good and not feel bad and the score often becomes a source of anger and frustration, leading to a tense performance. For the Authentic Tennis player, while tennis is a game that the score matters, it is kept in a broader perspective. The score has tactical considerations but the game is played in the present moment, rather than obsessing over the score. The Authentic Tennis player's emotional state stays on an even keel neither getting too high or too low. The middle or neutral path allows the emotions to flow freely, so there is a constant state of well-being.

6. **Mental Program/the voice of judgment.** The ego tennis player judges experience in terms of right or wrong and good or bad. This conditioning has taken place since we were young children. This voice of judgment often creates an internal battle where your conditioned program becomes your own worst

enemy. Judgmental thoughts like I am terrible, I stink, horrible shot, and how can I be playing this poorly, impedes the body's ability to relax. Judgment is just another name for resistance to what is. All resistance imposes tension on the mind and body. The Authentic Tennis player mental state is one of mindfulness and non-judgmental awareness, creating a mind body harmony. This mental release of judgment allows the body to relax naturally as a mental release always triggers a physical release. The Authentic Tennis player freedom from judgmental thinking allows for freedom in the stroking process.

7. **Opponent being much weaker or much stronger than you.** The ego tennis player views a weaker player either as a boring game or somebody that I can dominate, which makes me feel better about myself. The stronger player is viewed as threatening and is somebody that makes me feel worse about myself. Again the ego player is trapped in a duality or comparison mode that either acts as a catalyst to inflate itself or deflate itself. The ego player underestimates the weaker player, viewing the match as no contest and overestimates the stronger player viewing the match as torture. The Authentic Tennis player views the weaker and stronger player as having an inherent value, both being beneficial to play. The Authentic player uses playing the weaker opponent as a way to expand their game, working on all the shots to become a more balanced and complete player. The stronger player is viewed as a teacher whose court savvy allows the Authentic Tennis player to perform at their best and helps to

raise the level of their game.

8. **The unpredictability of the game.** The ego tennis player does not thrive on change because he/she works off of conditioned past programming. This past programming is not equipped to handle the countless possibilities of the moment. Miss-hit shots, an opponent changing game plans, poor line calls, bad bounces, and lucky opponent shots all tend to throw the ego player out of whack. The ego tennis player wants predictability so he/she can be comfortable and play in his/her past programming. The Authentic Tennis player, with their focus in the present is alert, relaxed, and ready for all possibilities. Being present allows the Authentic Tennis player to adapt to the constantly changing environment of competition. Only the now adapts to the now. The Authentic Tennis player responds to playing conditions by being flexible and adaptive.

9. **Playing against game styles that are problems for you**. For the ego tennis player playing against a style of player that they don't do well against is the same old scenario. The ego player's past programming does not allow them to sense a creative approach to handling a style of player that they don't match up well against. A common example is a player that constantly pushes the ball or hits loopy balls over the net versus a player that wants to hit the ball hard and low. The player who hits slow high balls makes it challenging for the hard low ball hitter to generate speed of stroke. If the ego tennis player is the hard low ball hitter they often end up going for too much and becoming

more and more frustrated leading to more errors. The Authentic Tennis player views this potential mismatch as an opportunity to explore a creative approach, leading to game improvement and the ability to handle greater numbers of playing situations. Take, for example, the previous high ball and loopy shot hitter—the Authentic player will search for creative ways of handling this loopy style of play. The Authentic player might adjust their own style of play by being more patient and looping some shots of their own. They might bring the loopy hitter forward in the court, taking them out of their defensive position and out of their comfort zone. They might move into the court and take the high loopy balls out of the air taking away time and creating an emergency situation for the opponent. The Authentic Tennis player views each opponent as a learning situation always benefiting them on their path towards constant improvement.

10. **How you might be feeling on any given day.** The ego tennis player dwells on the past and is often unable to let go of their daily concerns and problems. These daily concerns may include waking up tired, hard day at work, fighting with coworker or spouse, feeling under the weather, rushing to get to the match or waiting on the opponent to show up, etc. The ego player carries frustration, uneasiness and discontent with them into the match. The ego player often feels a hopeless situation and there is nothing they can do about it. The Authentic Tennis players move outside of their conditioned program and let's go of any concerns they might feel physically, mentally, and emotionally.

Letting go of concerns will allow the mind and body to be unified and to integrate experiences. The body naturally relaxes and emotions flow freely, the past does not condition the future.

Authentic Insights into Competition

1. You need your opponent. Appreciate your opponent's good shots. Sportsmanship is an integral part of an Authentic game.

2. The tennis game is about your ability to apply the racquet head to the ball, focus on the ball with no outside distractions.

3. Be mindful of the point of contact, it is the moment of truth. It is the point of connection in the present moment between the racquet head and ball.

4. Treat your mistakes as your teachers not as your enemies.

5. Play at your own pace or natural tempo.

6. Make a relaxed swing and solid contact your number one priority.

7. Enjoy the challenge presented by every ball, every opponent, and every situation.

8. **Play** tennis, don't treat it as a job.

9. Keep tennis in a broad perspective rather than a narrow perspective, it is not life or death.

10. Stay present and alert without being attached to what is happening.

11. Monitor your grip pressure to keep your stroke loose and flowing.

12. Use **breathing in** on preparation and **breathing out** as you

begin your swing, to feel a rhythmic flow and swing fluidity.

13. There is no need to react emotionally to your mistakes as you realize this is simply part of your past programming. Allow your emotions to flow. Stay in the middle and don't get too high or too low.

14. Be alert—the ball is a note; adapt your preparation, back swing and the speed of your footwork to the speed of the ball.

15. Treat the court as reference point, not a restriction.

16. **Feel** is process, the score is a result. Focus on the process not the results. Focus on the process and the results will take care of themselves.

Authentic Tennis has revealed the outcomes of following the path of the mechanical method and the Authentic path to your tennis swing. Although this book focuses on tennis, the word tennis in Authentic Tennis could be replaced with many words, i.e., Authentic Golf, Authentic Performance, Authentic anything.

Authentic Tennis is about more than just transforming your swing. It can be viewed as a metaphor for life and a vehicle for personal transformation and self-improvement. The aware-feel state of consciousness that will transform your tennis game can be interchanged with any area in life which needs attention.

While life is lived somewhere between the two extremes of mechanical or ego centered consciousness and Authentic or awareness centered consciousness, the state of feel is always present. What happens when you apply either one of these two paths to your life?

9 AUTHENTIC LIFE:
THE MIRACLE OF THE MOMENT

THE APPROACH OF AUTHENTIC TENNIS will create extraordinary results both on and off the court. Just like there are two paths to the tennis swing the holistic creative path and the mechanical programmed path, these two paths are also ways of experiencing your life journey. The mechanical path leads to the mechanical life. The mechanical path perceives life through what Authentic Tennis calls ego centered consciousness. Ego centered consciousness is a state where the mind is centered in the ego or who you think you are (ego-self). Ego-centered consciousness operates your ego's conditioned program. Thinking, judging, memory and reacting are all components of ego-centered consciousness. This consciousness operates outside the present moment separating you from all your life experiences. In living the ego-centered life, the future is merely a projection of the past. The past keeps manufacturing the future over and over again.

On the ego centered life path, experience is predictable, mundane, and ordinary. There is a kind of inertia that keeps powerful life transforming decisions from being made.

In the ego centered life there is a constant search for something to relieve the pain of existence. These include such addictions or distractions as alcohol, drugs, abusive relationships, food, work, sex, video games and personal image. The ego-centered life has bought into the concept that image and success is everything and that the end justifies the means. It operates in a state of struggle and sees no other alternative. The ego-centered life has many buried treasures or core values. They include survival, security, control, permanence, more material form or thought form, being of higher rank, seeking pleasure, avoiding pain and success in the material world. The core values of the ego and the ego-centered life negatively affect life on our planet. Such life issues as the environment, energy, health, politics and large corporations are negatively affected by the ego-centered life. The ego-centered life puts greed and personal success over what is best for life as a whole. This greed has led to the destroying and polluting of our natural environment. It has led to the lack of innovative ways to produce more natural and clean energy. Greed in health care has led to an over dependence on drugs and cost concerns, making treatment unaffordable for many people. It has influenced political leaders through payoffs by special interest groups and personal ambitions to be re-elected. The greed in large corporations, only caring about the bottom line—profit or loss, has led to treating people like numbers or machines that are either getting the job done or not.

The ego-centered life is leading to a more mechanical way of functioning, where advancing technology becomes the god. The ramifications of this, threaten all life on our planet. Technology has become a substitute for awareness. Cars can now sense road hazards that allow the car to stop without the driver paying attention to the road. The ego centered life manufactures technology that produces constant distractions such as computers, video games, Internet, texting and cell phones. These all steer people away from self-knowledge and their personal truth. The less that you are sustained by your own attention, the more you desire technology to distract you. The more you rely on technology, the less you rely on your own awareness and the natural evolution of your consciousness. Talk about co-dependency! The ego-centered life has become totally co-dependent on technology (mechanical evolution) and machines.

With all this technological advancement, it is essential in order for our planet to survive, that the consciousness of the human race rises to a level where technology is only used for the benefit of others. The ego-centered life has created a worldwide epidemic which Authentic Tennis refers to as ego-itis, or inflammation of the ego. **Ego-itis** covers up awareness, which is always present within the miracle of the moment when you shift outside of the ego's programming. Without a personal spiritual awareness and a sense of connectivity to the planet and to all human beings, the ego centered life and technology can become a destructive force. With the consciousness of the human race not evolving and with technology evolving at what seems to be light speed, we may be teetering on the threshold of disastrous consequences. However, there is a way out. Authentic Tennis welcomes you to the Authentic life!

The Authentic path leads to revealing the Authentic self and living an Authentic life. Authentic life perceives reality through awareness-centered consciousness, the miracle of the moment. Awareness centered consciousness is our natural Authentic state. It shows up when we begin to observe our thoughts without treating them and our beliefs as who we are. There is a source within our consciousness that is beyond form and the understanding of the intellect. The Authentic life through awareness centered consciousness bypasses the ego's conditioned program, illuminating a life of unlimited potential and possibilities.

The Authentic life through awareness centered consciousness is in constant contact with the present moment. Being-ness, non-resistance, creating, intuitiveness, and observation are innate qualities of awareness-centered consciousness. In living an Authentic life, the future is created deliberately. Awareness centered consciousness is a vehicle for the advancement of the human race. In the Authentic life path experience is exciting, unpredictable, and there are only extraordinary moments. On this path there is a constant joy and appreciation for the gift of life itself. The Authentic life is focused on greater self-awareness and helping others. There is a lack of struggle in the Authentic life; therefore there is no need to use drugs, video games, and alcohol for distractions. The Authentic life is focused on the quality of life for all human beings and it realizes that the process or journey is the end in itself. This is more important than any result or destination. The Authentic life moves effortlessly in a constant state of flow, not offering any resistance to what is or what happens in life. It is connected to source energy and the integral intelligence (God), the creator of our universe. The Authentic life values the present, faith in God, surrendered action, benevolence, selflessness, change, the formless or unseen, humility, all experiences, and serving others to our highest abilities.

The core values of the Authentic self and the Authentic life will only produce positive effects on our planet. Such life issues as the environment, energy, health, politics, and large corporations are positively affected by an awareness-centered life. The Authentic self realizes that there is a oneness of human connectivity and what benefits one benefits all. Benevolence or giving is the essence of the Authentic life. Benevolence towards nature will eliminate environmental problems. Benevolence on the energy front will lead to clean energy and make it available throughout the world. Benevolence in health care will lead to more holistic treatments and affordable healthcare for everyone. Benevolence in politics will lead to integrity and decision making that is in the best interest of everyone. Benevolence in large corporation will lead to a cooperative effort, working together to improve society as a whole over profit and loss.

In the Authentic life, consciousness is continually being raised and technology will only be used for the benefit of others. The Authentic life, perceiving reality through awareness centered consciousness, is aware of and accepts the ego. In the Authentic life, the Authentic self becomes primary and the ego plays a secondary role. The ego is like a barking dog in the back seat of the car with many desires; occasionally you need to throw the ego a bone but only if it can be done without hurting others. Keep your Authentic self, God-centered-with God at the wheel; your life will stay in feel. This is the miracle of the moment.

The Authentic life, perceiving reality through awareness-centered consciousness, realizes that change is inherent and inevitable. Every moment, the Authentic self is open minded, flexible, and ready to adapt to make the best of every situation. It realizes that everything in the universe happens perfectly, even though that level of consciousness and synchronicity cannot be understood by the ego or on an intellectual level of consciousness. The Authentic self appreciates both the "good" and the "bad" that comes to every human being. Life itself is a miracle and a gift too valuable to spend any time cursing it. The Authentic self has compassion for every individual on the planet. It realizes that we all go through a lot of struggle and pain and we all are on this journey, we call life, together.

There is a "paradoxical unity" to the universe, where things appear to be separate but in reality are connected. The Authentic life takes on a certain intuitiveness and synchronicity, where everything is seen as moving towards your calling. Life takes on an inspired quality as everything works toward the greater good of the entire human race. The Authentic life allows for a natural humility acknowledging the gifts of life, originating from a greater power and observed through the miracle of the moment. The Authentic life and the miracle of the moment evolve consciousness toward a more enlightened society, where the rising tide of consciousness brings up all humanity.

A MESSAGE TO OUR READERS

AUTHENTIC TENNIS is meant to be a reference for the differences between a natural swing and a mechanical swing, a natural life and a mechanical life. We realize that the game of tennis and the game of life are both played somewhere between the two extremes.

On one hand, we have all experienced the effects of being stuck in habits, which we seem to have no control over. On the other hand, we have all experienced our ability to be creative and transform certain areas of our life. Authentic Tennis presents the two extremes, mechanical and natural, simply to be able to recognize their differences and how those differences affect your tennis swing and life. We recommend making your natural state or Authentic self, primary in the mastering of the game of tennis as well as life.

Authentic Tennis does not judge or go against any method of teaching the tennis swing or playing the game.

Whatever makes you feel good about yourself, your tennis strokes and playing this beautiful sport, Authentic Tennis applauds.

ABOUT THE AUTHORS

BILL LEFKO is a professional tennis instructor with 40 years and over 40,000 hours of on-court teaching experience. He has a background in Transcendental Meditation, Neural-linguistics programming and a Philosophy/Psychology major at Austin Peay State University in Clarksville, Tennessee. He has spent his lifetime studying teaching styles and systems in the game of tennis. Mr. Lefko was a competitively trained and state ranked Florida junior player who played on full ride tennis scholarship at Austin Peay. He played as the number one player, singles and doubles in college tennis. He also played Contract Bridge (Life Master), on a national level for many years. He has taught tennis professionally in many states, Minnesota, Illinois, Indiana, Florida, New York, North Carolina, Tennessee and Kentucky. He and his wife now live in Hopkinsville, Kentucky, where Mr. Lefko has been teaching since 1996. He is currently teaching with his son Courtney Lefko. In 2003 Mr. Lefko received Tennis Coach of the Year honors for the state of Kentucky.

DANIEL BAIRD was a student of Bill Lefko as a junior tennis player. He is currently a professional tennis instructor who has taught tennis for the last twenty-five years, primarily in the Daytona Beach, Florida area. He has taught over 18,000 hours of tennis lessons to a broad range of students. Mr. Baird was a ranked junior tennis player in the state of Florida from ages 12 to 18. He was awarded the Volusia County High School Player of the Year in 1984 by the *Daytona Beach News Journal.* He attended the University of West Florida on a tennis scholarship. Mr. Baird has taken a wide variety of courses in the field of human consciousness and has integrated it into his tennis teaching.

ABOUT BLACK MESA

BLACK MESA IS a Florida-based publishing company that specializes in sports history and trivia books. For information about special discounts for bulk purchases, please email:

black.mesa.publishing@gmail.com

Black Mesa invites you to correspond with our authors:

AuthenticTennis@yahoo.com

www.blackmesabooks.com

CPSIA information can be obtained
at www.ICGtesting.com
Printed in the USA
LVOW07s1941091017
551769LV00028B/550/P